ABOUT THE AUTHOR

Steve Aylett is the author of several books including *LINT*, *Slaughtermatic*, *Rebel at the End of Time*, *Shamanspace*, *Fain the Sorcerer* and *Novahead*.

HEART
OF
THE
ORIGINAL

Originality, Creativity, Individuality

Steve Aylett

unbound

This edition first published in 2015

Unbound
4–7 Manchester Street Marylebone London W1U 2AE
www.unbound.co.uk

All rights reserved © Steve Aylett, 2015

The right of Steve Aylett to be identified as the author of this work has been asserted in accordance with Section 77 of the Copyright, Designs and Patents Act 1988. No part of this publication may be copied, reproduced, stored in a retrieval system, or transmitted, in any form or by any means without the prior permission of the publisher, nor be otherwise circulated in any form of binding or cover other than that in which it is published and without a similar condition being imposed on the subsequent purchaser.

All chapter subtitle quotes are from Steve Aylett books.

Typeset by Bracketpress

Art direction by Mecob

A CIP record for this book is
available from the British Library

ISBN 978-1-78352-091-6 (trade edition)
ISBN 978-1-78352-164-7 (ebook)
ISBN 978-1-78352-092-3 (limited edition)

Printed in Great Britain

For Lindsey

"Originality irritates so obscurely you may have to evolve to scratch it."
– Jeff Lint

CONTENTS

1	QUIT STALLING	1
2	LIKE THE FIRST TIME	5
3	EXOTIC ACCELERANTS	11
4	TREASURE	19
5	BLAST PATTERN	31
6	DEAD BY DESIGN	41
7	SALTING THE WASTELAND	49
8	THE THIRD CLOWN	65
9	THE FUTURE IS OBVIOUS	79
10	THE STITCH-UP	89
11	HEADS WILL ROLL	99
12	TOTAL CATASTROPHE WRITING	109

I

QUIT STALLING

*"The truly new invents
new guts for itself."*

IT'S AN OLD IDEA THAT IF WE GOT ENOUGH people spinning in their graves we could use it as a power source, a graveyard forming a turbine array. But since the spin-action depends on a preoccupation with other people's business and opinions, have you wondered how much energy *you* would produce?

Those who match nothing but themselves rarely notice the hairpin turns of external decree. They think in the rich syntax that results from living life in the wrong order. Fashion is a set of time's petty ordinances, local laws we submit to through inherited consent. In this environment truth is as loud as a photograph of a violin and originality both feared and slandered as legend. Nothing much interesting happens amid a conformity so innate it cannot clearly perceive or discuss itself.

Before the satirist Bierce threw his phone into

the furnace he talked about 'our resolutely stalled evolution'. A great one for affable scorn, he was admired to within an inch of his life. Like Twain, he had noticed that giving the same argument while wearing different trousers gives the illusion of varied insight. Those who claim that there are no more first times refuse to state when the last-ever 'first time' occurred. When did it all end? Others hold up old ideas in new clobber and claim originality. Anything to avoid creating the real thing. Combined with the historic policy of ignoring the first instance of any particular idea until it has spread enough to be restated generally, these approaches minimise the uncomfortable notion that an idea can originate from an individual. It's less disturbing to have a spider climb into your mouth than to have one climb out.

True creativity, the making of a thing which has *not* been in the world previously, is originality by definition. It increases the options, not merely the products. But while many claim to crave originality, they feel an obscure revulsion when confronted with it. They have no receptor point to plug it into. Attempts to force it result in the sort of fire that burned Tesla's wonder-lab to the ground. Repetition of familiar forms is preferred. The hailing of old notions as original lowers the standard for invention and robs most creative people of the drive to do anything interesting, let alone seek out the universe of originality which is waiting, drumming its fingers and wondering why nobody calls.

Raw thought is more available to those not stuck to the temporal floor. Thousands of 'what if the Nazis won the Second World War' stories are hailed as innovative despite the first appearing in 1937. In the mid-thirties Katharine Burdekin knew the allies would win the upcoming war but wrote a thought experiment about the alternative, *Swastika Night*, published the year Ayn Rand was busy plagiarizing Zamyatin's *We*. Randolph Bourne was one of the few journalists to suggest the First World War might not be such a bright idea and annoyed everyone by calling it 'the First World War'. It was supposed to be called the Great War or the War to End All Wars. Bourne was ignored because his opinion disturbed the narrative and because he was disabled. Another such figure was Simone Weil, the sort of goofy genius who'd fire all minds at a posh dinner and end up tucking the tablecloth into her pants and dragging everything to the floor.

But even those bold enough to accept the obvious have a preternaturally tenacious resolve not to venture beyond it. The absence of meaningful novelty doesn't help the boring catastrophe of modern times, congested with old deception. Let's blow our noses. Life is a moment to respond before we are repaid into the unknown. Find the strongest gravity, fold the world's edges into it and flip it inside-out like a dog's strange ear. Energy is merely the intermediary of oblivion's smithereens. Write every story as if it was your last, whether suicide note or proof of life.

2

LIKE THE FIRST TIME

*"How many times does a man have to shave
before his chin gets the message?"*

CERTAIN CEREMONIAL MASKS OF SUB-Saharan Africa portray expressions of astonishment and provide relief from having to repeatedly fake surprise at the same things — an energy-saving bliss reserved for the tribal shaman. Cultures which ban such masks through a prohibition against graven images are predictably scandalised at everything, including their own legs. The wearily exasperated looks on the faces of lions in the earliest cave paintings attest to Paleolithic people being constantly caught unawares by the cat's ferocious attitude. Woolly mammoths are also depicted as having been appalled to a standstill, rarely running or having a nice time. When shamans began portraying monster-jawed zigzag devils, antlered insect men and flying sharks to broaden everyone's horizon and ensure they wouldn't be dumbfounded by every development, the clan's hunters were still startled by the slightest sound. Fossil evidence suggests that early hominids had reinforced cheekbones to withstand being frequently punched in the face, and no wonder.

To the short of memory everything is unprecedented, and the rest are pressured to pretend. For the media to thrive, the uneventful must daily go with a bang using the Wolf-Rayet principle of massive gas and ferment gradually losing mass to the surrounding reality. Belong to the always-sudden world if you wish for shallow stress and lack of progress.

Roger Penrose's 2010 book *Cycles of Time* claimed that the closed-universe Big Bang/Big Crunch/Big Bang/Big Crunch repetition view was a new one, though it had been current for decades. We can use the same model to watch cycles of ideas, in which the same ones are claimed repeatedly as new. In the one-after-another closed universe model, no information is transmitted from one universe to the next. In the Cyclic Idea model of false credit, people present information and others later repeat it while claiming originality – after which someone else does the same, and so on. An equivalent to the 'crunch' node allowing the fraud is perhaps short attention span/memory, plus the desire to pretend to be absorbing new information without the small discomfort of actually doing so. It also drastically slows down the rate at which we can move on to the actually new. The relatively inexpensive necklace worn by Kali, Goddess of Destruction and Rebirth, consists of human skulls representing the alphabet used to create the universe. That these heads are empty at the node between one universe and the next lends support to the theory.

Repetition is now rife and instantaneous but in the past there were pauses, perhaps out of courtesy. In *Slaughterhouse Five*, Kurt Vonnegut has a time traveller watch bombs sucked intact into planes from city explosions below, then flown backward into factories where they are dismantled and their constituent minerals placed in the ground. Impoverished by his inability to copy other people's work, Richard Brautigan finally succeeded by using two sentences of Vonnegut's reverse gag in *So The Wind Won't Blow It All Away*, then blew his brains out. A few years later Martin Amis, a popular romance writer, inflated the idea into an entire book. (Many defend Amis, claiming he stole from *Counter-Clock World* by Philip K Dick.) The thin-spreading of a short idea is standard practice and it helps if the original author has died. A page or two of Octavia Butler's *Parable of the Sower*, massively dilated and diluted, makes McCarthy's *The Road*.

Many books are stolen vehicles with new plates

and zero torque. A lifted idea doesn't have the original's roots, the intense contract of energy between intent and responsibility. An imitation isn't earned because it isn't lived and hasn't the courage to be first. It didn't take two brains for the stegosaurus to support a solar panel array years before it became fashionable – just a true brain at one end and some nerve at the other. By the time solar power was rediscovered by Leonardo da Vinci his urge to 'think new thoughts and bring new things into being' meant that while other people were laughing at their own snot he was anatomising elephants and inventing the hang glider. Like a ligament statue he wore his own skull as a helmet and knew every inch of his innards. In his sizzling adrenalized mind, idea-shapes from diverse contexts magnetized together at angles which have no number or name, in the focused frenzy of what Zina Nicole Lahr called 'creative compulsive disorder'. He even managed to squeeze the classic Vitruvian Man out of an incident when a naked moron climbed onto his skylight. Born illegitimate, Da Vinci was freed early from the rusty harness of formal schooling and fell back on mere curiosity and honest observation of an infinitely spectacular universe.

The illusion of precocious innovation in the present derives partly from a foreshortened notion of timescale. In America, fundamentalist Christians claim the world was created 6,000 years ago. In Europe people drink in bars that are older than that. They discuss the in-built tragedy of those with an attention span of 300 years and a life span of 80. That difficult second novel was written in the 3rd century BC under the title *The Alexander Romance*. As far as we know the first was the 8th century BC Hebrew text *In the Day*, whose author couldn't stop herself developing a straight religious commission into a bitter, satirical potboiler. She set up the dialogue forms and 'show, don't tell' practice for everyone subsequent. Forty years after William Baldwin wrote the first English novel *Beware the Cat* in 1553, Thomas Nashe re-introduced the form with *The Unfortunate Traveller*, experimenting with portmanteaus and fertile all-inclusion to produce a tale with the precision of a jungle. The pen he dropped when poisoned by a herring was taken up over 300 years later by James Joyce to write his 'work in progress'. Maybe some information does pass from one universe to the next, compressed in the pea-sized node from which the latter unpacks itself. Joyce claimed that if everything else was wiped out, the cosmos could be reconstructed from *Finnegans Wake* – but he left out the evil.

3

EXOTIC ACCELERANTS

"Every sentence comes directly at you."

On Sant Jordi's day, Catalonians give each other gifts of books and roses in a celebration of literacy and love. If this were combined with the running of the bulls, the procession of the flagellants and the tomato-throwing festival, it would more closely resemble the tribulations of those trying to read – or love. I was trying to read Greg Egan once and was hectically attacked by a chimp. Videogames are meant to be an escape from the hassles of life but there too we are subjected to the violent stylings of vampires, cops and zombies. True escape would be an environment to explore without harassment or obstruction.

Words have the device-like detailed architecture of diatoms, and a glowing soul. A word will present itself as armatured with potential, as though with arms open, calling via your intuition to another word in another environment. You can enrich the stuff of life by bringing together two words which have never, ever been introduced to one another before. Perhaps because they dwell in different contexts or in the jargon of different disciplines, they are never held in the attention at the same time. Yet when put together, their cogs mesh as if they were made for each other and a massive amount of energy is released. This lexical love story is great to be a part of – how else would they have met without you playing Cupid? But when this manner of perception is habitual and constant, the vast transforming fields of idea-forms so effortlessly generated will tend to highlight the starved emptiness of a culture that replaces rich, consequential honesty with flimsy, contentless 'transparency'. When the figure zero came out of India it was meant to be built upon, not craved as entertainment. Yet rather than give the stillborn a civilized burial, booksellers display them for sale and entertainment like a macabre Victorian sideshow.

We've all encountered the sort of book that makes ordinary sense to most readers but perfect sense to those few whose minds revolve with the booming boomerang of the Milky Way. How much more wonderful, then, is a book that makes ordinary sense to no-one. There are thousands of so-far unnamed emotions. What might be expressed by an alphabet of 60 letters like Abkhaz, or the mere addition of the letter *else* or Grant Morrison's *triple-you*? We may compose a sentence that has more peptide bonds than it should hold.

A book may assemble a grammar that puts the world into bejewelled order, provides arcane nourishment or the charged sense of being an instant on the real road. Triangular dreams leave a galore scorch on the brain and heart. The million micro-tears a language undergoes are part of accident's great design – mad chance gave us the Brautigan-like oddness of the Bible's camel-and-needle's-eye image, the result of the Aramaic word 'gamla' meaning both 'camel' and 'rope'. It's a vision worthy of the balls-out crazy mayhem of Luigi Serafini's *Codex Seraphinianus*, a specific-rich art book in the tradition of the *Voynich Manuscript*. The joy of good surrealist art is that it puts you in a landscape where something interesting is happening at last. It reminds us of the time we idly wished for a head of three gyroscopic Ferris wheels in gold, black and red, or for a pea-pod to bear tiny faces which are at first startled and then flirtatious. Straight compositions remind us of a life barren of meaningful monkey business. The slantwise-stretched skull in Holbein's painting *The Ambassadors* manoeuvred the viewer to a point where they could read an inscription on the edge of the original frame, probably sarcastic and now lost. Conversely, some writing is less intent on what it says than on where your mind has to manoeuvre itself to understand it. Once in that place, forget the text and look around.

Giorgio de Chirico was a painter of strange late light and objects placed like chess pieces. Here are red earth, a gallery of arches, a tailor's dummy and the long black shadows which jet away from everything. It became an easily invoked cliché for advertisers and de Chirico himself lost interest, instead writing his first and only book *Hebdomeros*, a series of woozy atmospheres so diagonal it can only be a gateway to weaker books. Compared to this dodgy mess dashed off by a literarily clueless painter as he walked through a revolving door, most repeat writers have as much artistic ambition as a fossilized spud. Most books are reposts. Duplication paces the perimeter of pre-formed patterns. When the American genocide began, the invaders were free to smash upward into something new but instead made a preface of duplicating everything Europe had done, giving special emphasis to the garbage. This stale gauntlet reached a pitch with Henry James, who prayed before a silver semicolon and exercised a restraint so radical he imploded, taking a tornado of teak furniture and thousands of readers with him. A style prevailed that stated as little as possible in the most possible words. They even used this dross to paint over native masterpieces like the *Popol Vuh*. Among the few who ignored the colonial recapitulation was Walt Whitman, whose *Leaves of Grass* is so brilliant it'll pin you to your body. Some works are not dry tissue waiting for an observer to come and vitrify it. In a society which has amassed standards as a buttress against curiosity and invention, there are works with so many building code violations that a life of dazzling density finds its way in at every hole, shoots growing like turning keys. While others complained that the sky was nowhere near the window, Whitman opened the foliage door to astonishment. A bird could fly through it.

In the Medieval Irish novella *The Frenzy of Suibhne,* which starts with the slapstick of his clothes being accidentally torn away as he goes to confront a priest, Suibhne flips out amid a battle. But he is not a berserker and drops his weapons as an irrelevance – he becomes a wandering poet, still naked. Meant as a religious tract in which the poet's life is the result of a Christian curse, the author obviously loved composing the poetry that Suibhne chants on his travels. Such tracts are like the religious commissions of classical painters, who innovated strenuously to make the theme interesting to themselves in a way they could get away with. The most accomplished on this score was Hieronymus Bosch, whose idea of Paradise was a giant turkey baster surrounded by baffled wildlife. The egg-on-legs in his Hell appears a cosy abode and would be looked on with envy by the millions without shelter today. Suibhne became a Boschian bird but found no friendly shelter until Brian O'Nolan transformed him again in *At Swim-Two-Birds*. O'Nolan was a cast-iron genius and master of the Irish art of falling sideways into a sentence. He was also one for the time-honoured practice of inventing an author to provide commentary and to comment upon, a great way of getting rid of dozens of ideas per page – though for less ambitious writers such as Nabokov it merely creates one meaning inside another, like being dead inside a hospital. Publishers clamped their eyes shut to O'Nolan's *The Third Policeman*, another enviable Hell in which the participants are guaranteed basic amenities – and their eyes sprang open again after his straitened death. This venting of contempt prior to kindness, most graphically expressed in the military slaughter of civilians prior to candy distribution, is personified in the many pre-Christmas visitations of Saint Nicholas in Scandinavia and central Europe, during which he dresses up as a demon and rages through the neighbourhood, beating children with sticks, pelting them with coal and carrying them away in sacks to abandon in the middle of Spain. Children who already live in the middle of Spain are merely given a desultory prod in the eye, which they seem to accept with good humour. The Spanish tourist industry tried to sell this as a positive but couldn't really convey it – thus their reliance on a chaos of tomatoes, bulls and flagellation. The flipside to 'cruelty before kindness' is the south London practice of smiling at a man you are about to push through a plate glass window.

A book can bite you like a snake or unhook its jaw to digest you whole, slowly. It may be a rosebud clutched around a compressed infinity, an engine with all the scintillatory operation of a Tibetan thangka or a blessing from around ten corners in someone else's breakdown. One step aside waits a book like an alien fruit, a book like a rack of honeycomb, a book like a cognitive cathedral, a book that behaves like a liquid but explodes like a solid, a book that has pops and scratches like an old vinyl record, a book with tiny hook teeth, a stroboscopic book like an ocean species, a book that reconfigures between readings, a book of fused glass strata, a book you fall through quickly or an imprisoning book which slams upon you, its surface imperceptibly laughing. Dense, wordily mischievous ordeal novels like Moses de Leon's *Zohar* and Gurdjieff's *Beelzebub's Tales to His Grandson* were designed to overtask the rational mind to the point where it relents, leaving instinct to watch their colourful play of symbolic recurrences.

But heft has no inherent value. Roman consul

Lucius Opimius put a bounty on the head of reformer Gaius Gracchus of the head's weight in gold. The man who brought the head filled it with lead so that it weighed nearly 18 pounds. The book racket operates in a similar way, bloating its products with enough filler to result in books that are placid animals dangerous only for their great size. Luckily for the book trade, most writers haven't enough passion to ever burn out.

Bored by vertical and horizontal grammar, books without curves and so with a weak echo reflection, the weary individual is attracted at the very least to works so delicate the author must work between heartbeats, a literature that works through barometric variation. So the dog-in-a-sidecar joy experienced upon encountering even a single book which is active, that adds countless new elements to the literary periodic table, will swoon you into fizzing pools of rediscovered self-respect. To find them, be ravenous.

4

TREASURE

*"Imagine the horror of dropping into the world's throat
while trusting others' declarations above the
evidence of your own senses!"*

THE BODY FOOLS THE MIND AND HEART into facing in only one direction at a time. Truth is not separate or elevated – it inhabits the same space, like water in water. As much of it is behind us as in front. An animal like a dolphin with eyes on either side of its head and a large enough brain will think in several directions at once by experiencing an expanse rather than a line of direction.

You can loosen 'forward' imaging by regularly visualizing, with eyes closed, your body rotating to face backwards. It will feel very physical and at first the imagined body will want to snap back to face-forward – this is because your eyes instinctively swivel with the image and reach their physical limit. Eventually the revolving image encounters no resistance because the visual imagination has detached from the movement and orientation of your physical eyes. For visual thinkers this habit frees up an unused half-universe of imagination.

Real creativity is a ferocity of consciousness. It can be as small as the firestarter spark produced by those two words that have never been next to each other before or as stomach-rolling as translating yourself sideways into adjacent dimensions, a nearly-simple rotation of the soul which leaves you radiant with scorn and the precocious levels of seemingly casual opting-out only previously achievable on a framework of pumped, high-tensile resentment. You may even live a life with repercussions.

Many people have reached the edge of a component of truth and peered over into the deeps simply by noticing what hasn't been done before. It can be seen like the light which shows between the leaves of a tree. It's a rewarding game to poke around in the many spaces between those ideas, extracting the millions of thoughts which have not been expressed, but on the larger scale these notions appear cramped and hidebound. It's more fun to zoom out so that all that has been done before is a distant patch or speck – this gives you a massive space to play around in. If necessary the old speck can be used as a jumping-off point, if only to provide a point of orientation for other people. Listen to the billion ignored shapes that are scrabbling for attention – they're the interesting ones that release intense energy in gratitude or relief.

By the same token, when presented with a binary choice, a minimum of dignity demands that every option between the two presented be considered. But the line created between the two initial points can then be extended in both directions, rotated to sweep out a circle or used to triangulate outward into other possibilities. And at any point you can turn your whole mind around to look in the other direction for any distance. Quantum computers are starting to figure with all the superpositions between two states but they have trouble triangulating outside that line and factoring in everything else. For a real creative, terms such as 'think outside the box' or 'think the unthinkable' are limiting and baffling, as she cannot locate the fabled box amid the fertile infinite – a needle in a haystack, at best – and the second statement is gibberish. These slogans are designed to focus our attention on the box and the word 'unthinkable'. In fact the box is carried wherever the stone boat of 'brainstorming' voyages, where the air is ineffectively punched, where cruel shows of optimism and eagerness without content are rolled out often and to order. The active intelligence of a group doesn't settle around the level of the stupidest person in the group, but lower. If the devil existed, it would be in the form of a crowd. French po-mo analysts fearfully rejected the idea of individual human depth – when Nathalie Sarraute rightly observed that 'the deep uncovered by Proust's analyses ... proved to be nothing but a surface' she contrived to miss that this hinted at the true scale of what lay beneath. En-masse humanity's not-so-secret desire to be robotic and dispense with the complication of variety or the need to consider others has resulted in a culture in which psychopathology is the appropriate mindset. The wish to be inanimate – and the true individual's fear of those that are – turns up repeatedly in the fairy tales of Lucy Lane Clifford. *Wooden Tony*, *The New Mother*, *The Paper Ship* and *The Imitation Fish* are as creepy as a hen walking backward along a drystone wall. Those who mistake their religion or profession for full human identity are surprised when people treat them accordingly, though the benefit of the doubt is often granted. Many otherwise sensible people anthropomorphise the police. If you're a full-tilt human being you deviate innocently from the text and are not catered for nor acknowledged with accuracy. Flipped disregard is the slant sail used to tack into the wind.

The spatial method of finding ideas not previously expressed on Earth makes for a fun afternoon, but what of ideas not previously seen within the universe? An assumption about the universe is that everything is included, but its tendency to divide and particularise suggests it is seeking novelty – or straying that way despite itself. If your DNA were twisted into yet a further dimension, you could back sideways through all the abundance and decay of onrushing nature. Its interlocking reticulative elements are very available to pattern recognition, extraction and recombination. The fear of the intensity that comes with real creativity, that house tornado in which intermeshing components roll and radiate in collisions of velocitous bliss, is a pretty good gauge of your final creation's power. Heaven is hard to be around. Put the reader in the nosecone of the rocket. Human-built space trophies generally have the styling of a decade or so past by the time they leave the launch-pad because there's such a long development lead. But ideas are fleet, a controlled tempest of phosphene perspectives that have your eyes pinned open, making you forget to eat or breathe until the storm breaks and you hang what you've got.

Free of fashion or lobbying, the authentic from-the-ground-up thought of the individual births the original. Most of those who argue for the disengagement from whatever fads and laws have been concocted locally are still stuck to the temporal floor. It's a greater distance around than across a circle, yet it may take longer to cross. Outside of present time, it's easier to see reality is a constant, not an exception or interlude. Those who lobby for one mistake or another to have historic landmark status are wasting their energy. It's not only ignorance and cowardice which led to historically bad choices being repeated, but the lack of genuinely new options being introduced. Wisdom comes from an angle that can't be pointed to because it includes stored time. Even passive pattern recognition over decades can yield a realisation as slow and unlikely as a giraffe, and as harmless. Some truths gather like dust and can be blown away as easily. By retaining every direct observation and not letting others erase them, the entire canvas gets filled in. This isn't a tricky angle but the hinge of honesty. One of Sophie Scholl's White Rose leaflets quoted Lao Tzu: 'The wise man is therefore angular, though he does not injure others; he has sharp corners, though he does not harm; he is upright but not gruff. He is clear minded, but he does not try to be brilliant.' This comes so close to the truth that it's hard to believe he didn't know it. An angular personality is unlikely to align with the spin of the mechanism. But such people are too calm to be taken seriously and any attention they do get is either the humouring of an eccentric or as short-lived as the fad for chuckling which occurred after the freeing of the Russian serfs. Tough out the fake years and don't let the times waste your time.

It should have become easier to recall past errors since we began storing information outside ourselves in order not to have to remember absolutely everything internally. In the days when homes were heated by specially-installed swarms of bees, Saint Ambrose's ability to silently read and remember was seen as proof of his enhanced powers, and early attempts at mobile devices in the form of portrait miniatures thrived for centuries despite a marked lack of fresh content. However, since the storing of data externally became a second-by-second digital activity, the great majority of us have actually been thinking less, despite the large head space that our digital clouds have freed up. Whether this is a temporary tidal effect or we'll continue to think in our devices rather than our selves remains to be seen. Today it seems the brain is rapidly becoming a vestigial organ. Those whose minds are still functional are treated like the human survivor at the end of Matheson's *I Am Legend* – a disquieting throwback not to be trusted. There are precedents – since it no longer needs to move around much after attaching itself to a steady rock, the tunicate sea squirt eats its own brain. This cavalier attitude is not shared by all living things, however – an entire nervous system was found intact in the seemingly cheerful fossil of a great appendage arthropod, an extinct group of joint-legged creatures with large claw-like appendages protruding from their heads. Yet when Strindberg, a playwright whose own forehead resembled a fork-lift, was arrested for injecting morphine into the hanging apples of a tree, the arresting officer never had any serious intention of understanding his idea about plant nerves. Perhaps the cop was a religious man who didn't like the queasy idea of the Eden apple being a balled ganglion. The owl, too, has been a symbol of wisdom and doom, causing civilisations to furtively fear that wisdom entering by one door will push them out the other. Real owls are not very clever, however, and compensate for this with eyes the size of intake fans and huge bodies filled mostly with air. The truth of their condition allowed the city of Leeds to feel safe in sticking three of them to their coat of arms, along with a dead sheep in chains.

The notion of morphic resonance states that an idea or behaviour conceived in one member of a species can then arise in others at a distance, and it may be that the decision to ignore certain ideas and inventions is transmitted in the same way. A consensus is arrived at without overt communication. Like a slow crowd in which one person wants to move fast, it seems that culture will not allow an idea to affect it until it considers its 'time has come'. Yet crowds move slowly even when everyone in it wants to move quickly. The notion that culture's velocity is artificially throttled has persisted because the effects of conditions laid down by authority are clearly observable. Practical application raises the theory that an idea isn't taken up until it has mass, yet it's known that the least substantiated notions can take hold for centuries. Creative efflorescence itself is muted for centuries at a time. Such conservative, bland periods of culture are presumably meant to serve some purpose, like a sort of fallow period between crops. But it looks falsely imposed, unnaturally extended and applied with aggression, a famine as deliberately engineered as those of Lytton, Stalin and the World Bank. It seems a lot to do with fear, and not a justifiable fear – a shame because it wastes years of people's lives. In a flat time it can be hard to detect the point at which things begin to run in reverse. Historian Heribert Illig resorted to writing off the early Middle Ages, concluding that it must have been invented by mediocre scribes.

Perhaps in a universe where it's purported that every action will have an equal and opposite reaction, massive creative effort is bound to provoke its opposite. But the absence of any response at all is puzzling. In leaving stacks of evidence with ex-girlfriends, using a friend of his sister as a cut-out and looking exactly the same in every disguise, famously boring bomber Carlos the Jackal was effectively turning himself in. His wry amusement turned to exasperation when it took two decades for the arrest to take place. A message requires intelligence in the receiver. Whatever the process, just as the established speed of light is not accelerated by the speed of an object emitting it, civilisation is not automatically affected by the simple existence of an idea somewhere within it.

When Edwin Abbott Abbott wrote *Flatland* nobody saw it coming except Charles H Hinton, who had written the source material. Hinton created a 4D eye in his mind by memorizing a block of space and placing any object he saw within it, perceiving precisely what space it occupied. This process of 'casting out the self' was explained in his 1884 *Scientific Romances*, along with stories and essays in which he discussed dimensions one to infinity and the joy of 'the grasp of varied details of shape and form, all of which, in their exactness and precision, pass into the one great apprehension'. His novella *Stella* is about an affair with a woman whose refraction index is equal to air, rendering her invisible. His real romantic life was just as problematic, as he believed in marrying everyone he loved. Arrested for bigamy, he fled from England. He claimed he could walk through walls and repeatedly demonstrated the exploit at teahouses in his newly-adopted home of Japan. Moving on to America, he invented the baseball gun, which was basically a black powder cannon firing a ball at incredible velocity at the cowering batter. He died in 1906 while raising a toast to female scientists and his dimensional skylarking was forgotten so as to be devised by others at a more appropriate time.

Transdimensional thought is often interpreted as alien transmission, as when Anna Kavan was Zebra-struck in the 1940s and Philip K Dick had his Zebra contact three decades later. The same desperation to deny that human beings can think it up themselves led initiates in the gnostic gospel *Allogenes* to merge with a tutelary upper race by intoning its signatory insect sound and to the McKenna brothers doing the same thing 17 centuries later. In addition an idea may carry more than a taste of its origin, getting bogged down in biography and never being developed to a point of real application. Its champions are in awe of its limited inventor. The Buddha, in his journey from spoiled prince to chubby icon, learned that awe was a blockage. Admiration can be informative and useful but awe shuts down creativity in a stunned white-out. For instance the compelling value bestowed on a piece of art when it's suppressed can slow down the speed with which it's digested, acted upon and moved beyond. The awed mind enters a sort of tonic immobility, as some animals do when threatened or stroked on the nose. The male of the spider *Pisaura mirabilis* will give gifts and play dead to avoid the wrath of the female, a behaviour also seen in human males. Awe and reverence reduce a life to the token incrementing of earlier notions. Tinkering makes a fortune in echoes, the sort of success toasted with champagne in which the bubbles go downward. Ideas are approached with the strange need to square them with everything that exists already and reviews are read as if afraid of art that arrives unescorted. When the smart but chronically unimaginative control the narrative, dusty psychedelic mapping and the boring moorings of scripted countercultures are the only alternative most people discover. But these exist already. Look elsewhere.

The *creacionismo* movement believed a poem should be a new living thing which added to the world, rather than a reflection or description of it. For several years such tulpas were let loose upon Spain, causing horses to rear up and then simply come down again, a duplication of effort which tormented municipal planners. Inlibration works in contrast – for Muslims the *Qur'an* is god, a fixed point as god's creation goes on around it. The always frivolous Catholic church does a similar thing with biscuits. Religious strictures against creativity create the consolation of precocious exegesis and the offshoot of laws which are improbably human and strikingly male. For some, belief is lodged too close to the heart to be removed safely. In the wise such decrees move nothing, the urge to obey or be scorchingly contrary having worn to a powder and blown away.

5

BLAST PATTERN

*"The best way to get into something is
to think of it as mischief."*

IT IS NOT AN ORDINARY WORLD, EACH hair of grass a copy of the other. Before the fractures of continental drift, Earth held a single land mass shaped like a giant ultrasound of the creepiest baby in the galaxy. It was an accurate forecast. It now swarms with loud flightless birds that no longer speak in their own words. Early hurtlers sheared the wings off their philosophy, leaving them behind for others to try on.

From Lucian's *True Story* onward, writers have been populating the moon with avocadoes, giant spiders and severed heads, as if to keep such horrors at a distance. But it wasn't until Johannes Kepler's *Somnium*, with its understanding of gravity and comparative lack of larking about, that they transitioned from fantasy to science fiction. The moon was still a way to wish society's disappointments to arm's length, however, as in Campbell's *The Moon is Hell*. The gargantuan quantity of fact and consequence denied and evaded by human beings must go somewhere, and may constitute dark energy, the mysterious gear thought to compose 70 per cent of the universe. Thankfully most of the universe contains no pain receptors. These exist in great density on Earth as either deliberate torture or a measuring station. The greatest concentration is in a species which cannot stop lying and yet clings to the desperate insistence, in the face of all evidence, that there are really only seven stories. Their dictum of business is to sell people what they are already buying. True innovation and its dissemination are blocked, delayed, punished and obscured by the culture of the hour. In this hell, true creativity can only be an act of intense mischief.

Terence McKenna talked about the artist or shaman as someone deputized to take on and express all the weirdness in a society – it has to come out somewhere so this seems a good release system. Today those deputies see it as their duty to prevent anything genuinely weird getting through, at best expressing only former weirdness released long ago and since blanched of its power. How will the real thing come out? Where will the vivid go? Curiosity or hindsight tell us it will go wherever the most people are not looking.

In the pantheon of archetypes, only the trickster

doesn't run on rails – it zigzags across others' stories, self-starting and unreactive. It was first delineated, in fact, to contain 'everything else' which scholars and ancient storytellers couldn't manage to think up and symbolise in the other archetypes. Since these scribes were chronically unimaginative, the bulk of the universe's more interesting facts and possibilities ended up in the trickster. Those exiled from the dead arena revel in the fertility of their damnation – the glory of unconditional weirdness, with its generosity, exuberance and lateral grace. The supposed weird fringes are the only place honesty can find asylum. Real shock is honest. One cannot be sly and shocked simultaneously.

Popular lifetimes are like the frantic cartoon you see if you use a Tarot deck as a flick book. It's different each time you shuffle but there's always a blood-sugar panic of powerlessness. Destiny is a dead lightbulb from the room where you were born. The discarding of inherited scripts gave rise to the highwayman Gamaliel Ratsey, performer of gleefully baffling robberies in which he threatened to 'compare' himself to anyone who didn't comply. The trickster slides parallel to bewildered definitions. Alexandra David-Neel, John Whiteside Parsons and Isabelle Eberhardt slipped between divisions without being aware of them, resulting in lives other than stock footage. The painter Chaim

Soutine was attacked by his sitters, a hazard exacerbated by his belief that hanging offal everywhere would speed him to glory. Every landscape he painted flexes and flares with an effort to leave the canvas, in contrast to many of his contemporaries, in which it seems a slash of paint is caused by the canvas trying to get away. A system is never so good that it couldn't be improved by a hen on the rampage. A hen displaying sustained rage and destructive disdain amid any human circumstance – though not toward it – is a hectic gift from Mother Nature.

Storytellers tend to neuter trickster figures for longer works. Wu Cheng'en tied Monkey to a boring priest for his *Journey to the West*, fearing that the adventures of Monkey unbound would lack a structure people would recognise. The superconservative Marvel movies rewrote Loki as a villain so clueless his greatest achievement was to make the Hulk seem interesting. A life or text in which every link is spelled out will be expunged of mischief, leaving no task to the mind. We are left with countless accounts of reactive remnants and records of mitigation, shrivelled from the get-go. It's such an effort for ear-breathers to get their heads around trickster behaviour that they lazily short-hand it as zany and hyper, and thus in accord with a world of scared extroverts. But the real thing is the least hysterical in the room.

We've seen that the command that there must be nothing new under the local sun has even led people to blame their own ideas on external forces, in the same manner that people are expected to ask themselves 'Who am I?' and earnestly pretend they don't know. All of which leaves a person unable to speak in his own words and expecting acclaim for old outrages as if unaware of double jeopardy. Pain or pleasure habituates when stationary, becoming ineffective – the Sirens found they had to frequently modulate their song. The true work may be a mile of dovetailed atoms in which each idea is one operative molecule. With this it may be possible to inject an anthem intravenously. How does a paper book work on zero voltage? By spinning unequal drives, a volume may constitute an artificially-generated black hole, its incandescence eroding the time that holds it. Satire ensures a book is not a passive experience but an active one requiring the reader to lean into its curious machinery. Snagged and dragged in, it's not the end but a beginning.

Voltaire, a man with a heart like a boxing glove, who chose a pen name like an electric shock, exercised such unfashionable integrity of thought he threw the race into a sort of asymmetry. Later in life Voltaire conceived of a book that would delineate the same cosmic negligence which today provokes a million suicides a year. *Candide* displayed humanity in all its polyphonic justifications and retractable morals, its inequality and poverty as bad as anything seen in our own time, and the pious puffed-up with humility. The only things that are hard to believe are the interlude in El Dorado and the fact that the characters survive their various ordeals. It's not often one encounters such openness in an adult. The speaking of human truth seemed a precocious innovation and always does, as it's the thing that's no sooner dug up than buried again to provide amusement another year. Good satire acts as a reality agonist, flooding the brain with common sense and the heart with honesty – a bloody relief.

Unlike the sloppy sarcasm that has now taken its parking space, satire is a set of very specific mechanisms. The simplest is the bait and switch, whereby a principle is stated with which all can agree, and which is then applied to the 'wrong' situation to show a double standard. The end of the sentence is the detonator for the truth the reader has already swallowed – it's too late to cough it up. At its best this chest-burster method is amazingly messy and annoying, and has people backpedalling so fast they red-shift due to the much-loved Doppler effect. In Voltaire's *L'Ingénu* the protagonist gives his first confession and naturally assumes that the priest will likewise confess to him. A struggle ensues. Voltaire specialised in innocents who took folk at their word, their effect as unsettling as the more knowing holy sarcasm of Dario Fo's St Francis and the clarifying angel in Twain's *The War Prayer*. Such succulent reason studded with consequence amplifiers sets up a beautiful golden mechanism with light running all through it, a pure but human honesty machine that burns along like a vimana.

Satire engines of a certain type 'conclude' a civilisation and so bring to light what sort of knot it's swung itself into. History is not a string of burnt flags. Mere history could not assemble such irresponsible masters decade after decade. They assemble themselves, pausing only to bite a sparrow's head clean off in an atrocious foreshadowing of future difficulties. Humanity changes its shirt, religion, phone, but not its nature. Firearms are needed for a full-dress version of its philosophy. American friendly fire is rightly feared throughout the world. But the comparison of monsters with one another does not decrease their population. Evil clarified remains evil, and those who delineate it get their hands dirty. The extraordinary *I, Pet Goat II* glistens with the evil it portrays. It's hard to have a life on the slope of the gravity well. Sloths take weeks to digest the toxic leaves they eat, with everything else slowed almost to a stop by the process. Meanwhile they're sitting ducks for predators that they must disarm and discombobulate with the biggest, wettest eyes and cutest faces on the planet. This has never been an option for me, since at the best of times I resemble a snail which has been stamped on by a pathetically sobbing barber. Luckily, satire is not the mere circumnavigation of a lie.

Satire discharged at a low trajectory may have the largest target area but the blowback is an understanding of its shallow effect. Multiple targets and absolute precision create a richness of specificity, an exquisitely tooled tableau of chinless wonders and crawling chefs. It's easy to make it look like an accident. Catalytic satire may expend no energy while unlocking it in the space it occupies. At its best its very existence and placement is a confounding artefact which sends everything around it into silence and absurd defence. In this it resembles large portions of nature, the implications of which must be ignored if a person is to engage in society. When elephants were used in battle, their riders tried to blur the line between themselves and their powerful steeds by dressing them in trousers identical to their own. In the day of the armoured tank this practice has ceased. Such modest admissions of human frailty are relatively new – as recently as the Second World War the US navy used dazzle patterns to make observers believe its ships were a more radical shape or that those on deck had snazzier hairstyles.

Today the individual soldier pretends to no greater power and films the evidence on his phone.

Voltaire has now forgotten he lived among a million clowns. It turns out his genius was consecrated to a type zero civilisation. He wasn't dumb enough to think that evil dissolves upon discovery, but he had his hopes for the future. Politics has long since found its way into every corner of government and crime is the only remaining way of making money commensurate with one's efforts. Saints are worked to weakness in empires of stupendous dupes and panoramic scaffolding. Its roots reaching under the dusty valve tomb of television, the internet was established as a safe tantrum arena while ensuring that the desire of many artists to be appreciated for their art and also to be left alone to create it was finally irreconcilable. The muse of satire is called Thalia, who rhymes with failure, as does her name.

In the middle of the 20th century, palaeontologists found a small dinosaur fossil *Coelophysis* inside a larger fossil *Coelophysis*, and wondered whether it was a case of gestation or cannibalism. The same question will occur to those who find human fossils in the ruins of our cities.

6

DEAD BY DESIGN

"When a monster passes, we take it for another whose favourable opinion we must seek."

LAZY OBEDIENCE IS A UNIT OF ENTROPY. Entropy is high because there are countless dismal acquiescences to fall into and only one or two very focussed and specific manoeuvres by which to maintain yourself. Those who burst out thinking in public encounter not only sarcasm and physical aggression but a total lack of legal recourse. It takes skill to 'pass' among the standing dormant while remaining alive. This zombie camouflage involves more than merely looking happy. In a past when the options available were disappointingly unimaginative dares or the heaven complained of by Jesus, most people had to blame their interesting remarks on demonic possession, however seldom these might be. And then the inconvenience of death or exorcism. Rasputin was dubbed the 'mad monk' because, in times as conservative as our own, he sat down on one chair and rested his legs on another. He repeated this 'two-chair jamboree' in several venues, and the practice was later thought to be the source of his mystical powers.

It's been said that a tree is known by its fruit, and this has become a world where it is a risk to be known. Keep the light behind you and they won't see you're thinking. You might also pass off an original notion by prefacing it with 'It's an old idea that...' or 'It's a cliché that...'. You've shunted it into the past, rendering it presumably banal. Hoaxers used to pass off narwhal horns as those of unicorns. A greater gift would be a unicorn horn passed off as that of a narwhal and the subsequent realisation of its worth as it turns gold over the fireplace.

Another strategy is to adopt a standard-issue boil-in-the-bag wackiness such as pink spiky hair – this will be accepted and people will feel they've done their dutiful work of scanning for individuality and found nothing. You're hiding in plain sight. You could even out-die them by agreeing fiercely, enthusiastic to the brink of assault. Such ferocious assent is startling and will disconcert long enough for a getaway. But remind yourself that benevolence may create an initial fight-or-flight response in others, followed by long-term suspicion and hostility. These consequences are the source of legends about curses incurred by meddling with a mummified cadaver. Take fear, as when an insect starts to bulge.

It's better to bring 20 invisible things into the room than nothing at all. But those billions of quiet neutrinos give you an alien flavour. It's uncanny how they know there's something not quite right about you – an unidentified heat signature. Like the pod people in *Invasion of the Body Snatchers*, they can detect some sort of inner lifespark and will alert others in their anxiety. If asked, they could not explain why they are threatened by your sinister equilibrium, the fact that you live in a freight elevator and are growing a zebra orchid in the casing of a plastic radio. Disagreement, to a true believer, can be easily tolerated. The boundaries of organised religion are military.

Do not accept responsibility for their impression of you and don't overturn the whole scheme to accommodate their theory. It's useful to remain silent when someone wants to be interrupted. To the commercial doctrine that a person is a territory with no worthwhile exports, only imports, the individual who does neither is an abomination – the human equivalent of a Dyson Sphere. The skin conceals collisions of light and ability. A secret can be an energy source, a red organic battery. And by the time the secret's fully out, the battery's spent – but it's served its purpose. The comfort of deception – it keeps the deceivers busy and satisfied.

They could be doing something far worse, perhaps with monkeys. There may come a time when even the most masochistic of innocents find no more room for guilt and the swim of accusations can no longer be absorbed. These noises of a sudden have no significance and must go elsewhere if they desire a home. It may be years, if ever, before the accusers notice that a change has occurred. Solace is not loaded, it tends to be simple. For those who even breathe out of sequence, may they achieve what was said of Weil: that she erased her name but left it underlined.

But why hide? How expressive of life is a portrait in the attic which gets more colourful and smart as the outer you is desaturated by society's baffling pressure to over-react? Scandal bores because it requires a foundation of consensus. In this unfulfilling masquerade there are many whose personality is a periscope, the real thing thriving beyond observation, and enough real idiots that your sham idiocy isn't required. Do something else. Interactions with neurotypicals can be a study in why people behave the way they do around originality, and the fun you can have making people behave that way. To them you may appear as radioactively terrifying as an angel. A price to be paid for individuality is the abandoning of approval – actually a reward in itself. Robert Ingersoll and Yang Chu were weightless in their indifference to the false frenzy their words generated among the dogmatic. When the audience threw fruit at Charles Ludlam he'd catch it in his mouth. You may find the grace that fills those who fall upward into the epic win of exile.

It's inevitable that upon those rare occasions of encountering an original notion externally, you will start drooling amid blowing fuses, the abyss at your side intermittently visible and scaring the unwary. The rest of the time, it's all you. People will be happy or stricken to see each hacking cough release a green butterfly with the body of a stuntman. Arrive in a stupid badger-faced biplane with five adrenalin pens hanging off your forehead. Arrange for your arms to be already windmilling as you enter a room, if possible knocking out the teeth of a spoilt child. Retrieve a hemisphere of flowing mercury from your inside pocket and gaze at it in an attitude of ferocious, twelve-bore self-pity. Leave unacknowledged your coffee-coloured antlers and wings like the ghostly bones in the X-ray plastic used to press Soviet samizdat records. Stand pelted with angry finches, ashen-visaged in a moth-shot coat, thoughtfully scratching someone else's chin. Go accompanied by a man-size chef with a parabolic face, carrying something which appears to be a torpedo. When asked your opinion, squander all good will in a blast of neutrality. Start your case from a position extrapolated way forward as if deliberately to annoy. Release a scuttling thing found in an undersea volcanic vent. Count backwards with increasing volume, looking tense. Whisper spookily of 'the boy in the floor'. Use your own blood to scribble valence values on the wall while visibly taking on the distance colours of a mass card. Is it anything more than childish honesty? The preening dead can inspire just as the spaces between packed spheres are a more compelling shape than the spheres themselves. Listen to them attentively, carving a quick wooden rendering of their gobs in action. Cradle a hapless shad which looks them in the eye during the full hour it takes to gasp its last. Push their 'oblique strategy cards' into a dimensional pocket in the air, your face wrinkled as a flower. Point easily at the blue gold ceiling as it becomes transparent to reveal a clambering unison of infinite madcaps. Disappear in every direction or rise in a smack of black feathers, leaving them with simultaneous frostbite and sunstroke. At the very least claim that your father made a living wrestling with a medical skeleton as upward of 70 people bet money and roared at him in a boiler room.

When relaxing outside the 'Goldilocks zone' of tolerated zaniness, your bespoke insecurities will make others' look all the more off-the-peg and cause an anxiety with no name. But it all too often degenerates into something done for effect or even approval. Faced with a race of technological predators with no self-control and a pretended fear of pretend rebellion, it doesn't take long to realise that solitude is unbeatable for congeniality. If it happens that you can run rings around them, that doesn't oblige you to use them as a focus. Do you have an obligation to fill a vacuum so total that lightning will innocently swerve to plug it at a rate of 400 victims per year? As a public service Nikola Tesla took time off from his busy schedule to manufacture ball lightning and ping it into the town, though as usual most of it headed straight for church. In the US most people evade the duty to question their government as stated by the founding fathers and are happy to be un-American. No point hanging on – Darwin waited before publishing his evolution ideas but people were still surprised. There comes a point of exhausted exasperation at one's every act meeting with blanket disapproval. The only sane course is to disengage. Subtract your weight from their calculations. But sudden absence creates a sonic boom – better to be incremental. To depart from the narrative is to disappear, if it's done right. Go the way of Bierce and Don Van Vliet. No one will see the look that passes between you. Medieval poet Francois Villon, repeatedly banished by the authorities, vanished at last when he wished to. The poet Ferrer Lerin quit the literary scene to study vultures in depth.

Thoreau's *Walden* is one big, beautiful restraining order. People are often corrupted by their desire for power or wealth. Has anyone ever been corrupted by their desire to be left alone?

When excluded from human society, don't stop to get it in writing. You are free.

7

SALTING THE WASTELAND

"Templates can't stand a masterpiece."

In the Bon tradition, a tulpa is an object created through sheer focused thought. Buddhists call it a *nirmita* and Lewis Carroll called it a *phlizz*. The compressing of ideas into books for subsequent release can generate a small-particle tulpa swarm if done correctly. You'd expect the most boring phenomenon to therefore be the least probable, but it turns out this is the only one anyone bothers with. Its lowest form is the golem or academic, someone locomoted by others' words on their brow and incapable of creating anything from scratch. Diplomas cover the walls like custard pies and a billion ideas fail to conceive. True creativity is a soliton wave, perpetual unless obstructed. It's reasonable that the Prayer of Jabez boils down to an encoded plea for god to simply leave him alone.

Like any valuable commodity, the most dangerous time for an idea or philosophy is during transfer. All forms of damage, manipulation, theft or loss can occur as it's being expressed from one person to another and this may sometimes be deliberate. Even fire is fragile when it's small. The young Buckminster Fuller was stumped when his teacher represented infinity with a shabby line capped by an arrow, finding it more representative of limitation and expired curiosity. Mired in formal education, Fuller started his career popularising other people's ideas, such as Walther Bauersfeld's geodesic dome, before gaining the confidence to head off on his own with synergetics, an idea he'd carried around in a perforated box for years.

When Walter Benjamin saw Paul Klee's painting *Angelus Novus*, which portrays a sheep's head on the body of a hen with cardboard legs, he called it "the angel of history", a fairly astute view considering the way history is taught – without connections, cause or effect. In keeping with the policy of incoherence and surprise, incidents are inserted without warning into the faint flow of things – no root or growth, and denied even the oxygen required by that most sarcastically unresponsive of house guests, the airplant.

For many, school is an experience of such toxicity and destructiveness that it is merely a thing to spend the rest of their lives recovering from. It serves as aversion therapy or a system of encapsulated samples introduced to stimulate antibodies against creativity or knowledge. The antibodies cover koans in commentary, exclude the wrong-note realities of life and seal the spirit against brilliance. Teachers who present the promise of a full-blast-on-all-cylinders nerve array prove as disappointing as ornamental berries. Some adopt the 'stern cadaver' style of teaching, marked by a contentless disapproval of humour and a perverse pressure to learn reluctantly. They are professional mourners.

In this freezing inferno, a child grows with the certain knowledge that she is only one of billions. Those who speak of the golden age of community overlook those ages when it was possible to be left alone. Amid an infringement so total as to be superimposition and the hobbling effect of peer hysteria, it is not done to remark on the obvious: that it helps kids to get used to boredom, obedience to people who are wrong, and the rewarding of the loudest. To scold is to bore with restriction, which in a secure kid will feel like an urge to go and explore. Indignation in a child provokes mirth or disgust, but what is the contribution of a child who never felt indignant?

The unfortunate honest try to play along by building a barrier against truth with Tetris-like efficiency, only to have the wall immediately disappear. For many savants and synesthetes, ideas and philosophies have a shape, colour and operation, and this perception is an instant means of knowing their quality. If an argument has a hole in it, there's a visible hole. It makes the flatness of fanatics as apparent as political sleight of hand. It's even possible to design a hole into an argument to lure someone beyond its darkness, like the impossible shafts and missing walls of the vessel in Hans Henny Jahnn's *The Ship*. Among clairevidents the purpose of certain ideas is the shape they make in the mind – they are intended to be decoded in the form of higher-dimensional sculpture or schematics. Connoisseurs slip each other the raw texts like addicts of an unbranded drug. To most people the only clue may be a repeated contradiction making folds in an otherwise coherent narrative, or a bit of wiring that seems to serve no purpose. The addict will sense at once whether a book contains anything.

The child thinking along these lines looks around the schoolroom in dismay, and as this turns to disappointment and depression, the idea calcifies inside her like a stone baby, staying there until they are dead together. The same goes for the child thinking about snot. Hearts go numb with less commotion or recognition than a big break and are mourned too late or not at all. Lights are going out even now.

After ejection from a school, personality is determined by whatever happens to fill the hollows gouged out there. At the very least energy and years are devoted to compensation for the pulling and squeezing as the wound changes focus. One of the main consequences of today's infantilising culture is that the traditional denial of a child's sentient humanity has been extended to adults, especially in the workplace. Companies are now operated as if full automation has already taken place. Solutions vanish every second of every day and we will never know the geniuses lost to the cubicle or to cops in a burst of taser confetti. Occasional reforms pump out the remaining air – the Trilateral Commission began to reinforce the trend in the 1970s when it concluded that public trust in governmental authority had declined because American youths were over-educated. Rebalancing nature is like drawing an equator through a starfish. I did that once and it started shouting at me. No one entirely succeeds in getting bent back into shape.

But you can't always be sure what's rocking in the bomb cradle – raised by a mother like a whale heart, you can still spend a life guessing the weight of the world. A believer in truth, having dodged formal schooling, William Blake navigated complicated moralities as one would stride across a mosaic floor. His testaments to the great beyond are like one-shot tarot cards, hand-painted and human. Hoping to be reckoned with but finding no takers, his few commentators ran out of steam before they could get their act together. Blake meanwhile stood with the luminous endurance of a saint. He could have gone far and fast if he'd got any traction, but cultural flat-Earthers would look away for many more years, each like an eternity.

It can be interesting to look at those scarce cultures that have been entirely *honest* about not wanting anything different or very interesting. During the tacitly tolerated phase of *rumspringa* or 'running around', many Amish adolescents find that the regular world's pretence at encouraging imaginative individuality generates a stress they are unprepared for. Honesty is always a relief and saves energy. Faced with two restrictive cultures, most choose to stay with the one which is upfront about it and ignore any options beyond these two. Whether agreeable or contrary, they resemble cellular automata that alternate in binary and depend on neighbours' values. We've all heard the story of the man who wrapped a map around his head and then burst the latter like a balloon. Beginners in spatial thinking can write an idea, put it down and walk away while acknowledging all the adjacent ideas they're wading through – keeping a continuity of mind down the street and round the bend leads fairly soon into vivid territory. But for some a notional vertigo stops even the simple dropping of an idea to see where gravity takes it.

The apparent lack of receptor points for the original to plug into is only in people's minds. In the absence of fear, the mind has as many orifices as it wants. Yet even for the fearless, off-the-peg wackiness marketed as originality often serves as a prophylactic against the real thing – there's no need to try for something seemingly already owned. Many people defer the achievement of anything interesting to their offspring. This postponement may roll over for a hundred generations before either they stop pretending or someone finally accomplishes something and is frozen out of the family for being a weirdo. Some parents take delegation seriously and decide who the child ought to be before its fontanelle slams in their faces. Most adults who resist for a while the urge to delegate finally decide to dangle from their own past, disguising themselves as their earlier, living version. One kind of surrender masks another and the false epiphany of late-life political conservatism helps. In the curiosity of last resort, they find that in a whole life the meaningful events add up to a few days, or the length of a story.

Hermann Hesse's book *Beneath the Wheel* describes a child who is curious about the world but is under the control of people who understand none of the factors in that equation. Unlike many other writers deemed to be phase reading for teens and slackers on a zoned-out god safari, Hesse can be revisited and found more solid and viable than before. From his earliest days he studied the myth that so long as enough stupidities are convergent, there will be a viable civilisation. He doubted that the sun needed alibis or embellishment and wondered why tycoons were so boring. Basic stuff but fluorescent thoughts for a child stitched into a sailor suit. His elders tried to mute him with a course of opera appreciation and rote recital, or what today we would call attempted murder. He was honestly bewildered by the perfunctory topology of their beliefs. They had built churches for gossip and appeasement, tapering the congregants' preoccupations upward like the filament of a silkworm until the steeple's apex held a single pinched nerve. An attempt to throw himself on the mercy of the river saved him from those equally useless fates, standing speechless with illumination or draping around in contentless ennui. He'd got a fright and emerged irradiated. Something had changed in each door and each lock. He decided against being an author who adds not one new detail to the impressions we have already collected. The fool sleeps in the master's hand. Living out a life in the golden climate of creativity, he ended up telling stories in the ninth person and the subtemporal tense, exquisitely tooled narrative cascades with thousands of integrated components and the intricate valving of a chiton. It's an extravagant open system of wisdom well-spoken, as surprisingly broad and detailed and strokable as the iris of a sunflower. Though pragmatic as the python he resembled, culture had him seen as inscrutable as a cigar store alien. Deference, reverence or expected bafflement – these keep the content unexplored.

The historical Doctor Faustus is reputed to have been vindictively boring, perfecting the method in both silence and many words. Watching people and guessing at ingredients, he extruded the moment in all directions, wasting the time of everyone he knew. That's how he spent his gifts. Resources too often go to those with no imagination. There are those who think it unseemly that an individual without extensive 'formal' education might have risen to Shakespearian heights – far preferable an Edward de Vere, one of the landed gentry capable of evading in nine languages and possessing enough cash to screw up badly and fall arse-backwards into Christmas. It seems more fitting to some that great work should emerge from one who has had an approved programme of knowledge fed in increments to his incurious brain, rather than one who is actively voracious for any knowledge he can find, like a candle learning at both ends. It would shore up the conceit – not a fantasy because it's not actually desired – that precocious individual thought can be established mechanically by syllabus. Probably it's been argued that the man we know as Abraham Lincoln was not in fact the boy from Kentucky but a privileged landowner who used the poor dolt's name. The truth is not hierarchical. Those ravenous for knowledge chomp through it like ever-starving zombies, blood hanging from their faces.

Born and counting, Antonin Artaud studied the world as if facing his accuser, seizing and turning to account each street and field presented to him. He had a face like a wet kestrel and more worries than a shaved lion in a rental car. His appetite for honesty had him digesting his own bones. Many put his desire for a 'body without organs' down to the fact that his own were rubbish. He struck an attitude that no one could understand, wheezing like a hilarity. It's been claimed that Artaud's performances were kicked off by the writer rattling his limbic system in a hat and throwing it at the audience. It was then for the audience to remark upon whether he was entitled to do so. In fact his works were as closely appointed as daily life, a familiarity he then threw lopsided in five directions by introducing the nonconformist element of common sense. This put him out of favour with Breton, whose equational tirades and art deco synapses carried less juice than the moon. Artaud was soon booted out of the Surrealists for his position that lobsters belong in the sea and other notions troubling to the movement. His belief that there's no such thing as an amateur scream was unwelcome in a world where it's not acceptable to scream in company, irrespective of the pain level. Artaud hadn't learned such unspoken rules and never discovered where those mute lessons were held. In 1948 he recorded a spoken piece commissioned for French radio titled *To have done with the judgement of god*, a screeched diatribe on how to dance wrong-side-out and deliver Man from all his automatic reactions, punctuated with viscerally terrifying shrieks and hoots. France had only recently commenced the denial of their four-year Nazi collaboration and a copycat genocide in Algeria – this feral squawking of Artaud's didn't fit the bill. After one listen it was officially declared unfathomable. Enforcement was unnecessary among a crowd that could be depended upon not to bother anyway. Nobody could remember for a long time afterward that Artaud's mouth had distended into a sort of ribbed pipe like a duduk flute. In fact some of the shrieks heard on the recording are those of the sound engineers. And with his head now resembling that of a shovel-nosed sturgeon, it never fully recomposed itself. Doctors prescribed him enough chloral to kill him several times over, a measure which took account of his virulent desire to live. He died a month after the programme's censorship. It was thirty years before it was broadcast. Artaud's deathmask could double as a crowbar.

America, another empire with its heart in its jaws, observed the dead walking or hanging by a catgut thread of credit and wished none of their scratches of protest read into the record. Nelson Algren confounded these contortions by going up and asking. Uncle Sam valued decree above the facts at its disposal – Algren made a practice of allowing what was in front of his eyes to reach his brain without interference. Researching for a book called *Nonconformity*, he saw people listening to sermons that ended them; those lucky too late for it to help; the dead springs of those who had lost their faith and turned to religion; the strange tension of disorder at rest; police retribution and the nostalgia for a foreign threat since serfdom was rediscovered in the factories; kids carving Fibonacci forearms and bleeding in pulsed spurts; shadows pegging it to nowhere. In those days there wasn't much to it. America's fear of a dangerous naked democracy led everyone to shriek at truth with the bandages removed. Algren pointed out that there are few things less available for public use than a public statue; that it is possible to be simultaneously monumental and misguided; and that statues take a long time to die.

In a culture where it was patriotic to be guided

by alarm, Doubleday reneged on his contract. The grave kept Algren safe from gladness when *Nonconformity* was finally published, 45 years after he finished it. A topical book so recently old should taste like a dead firecracker but Algren created a system of gyroscopic ribs surrounded by 18,000 moving parts to power a summary incriminating government and its infantile finalities. Then as now, the authorities' pondering was so plainly outside the problem that they only reached the solution to its front yard. Critics abhorred Algren's pointing out flaws and proposing no solutions, on the odd grounds that a man unable to stop a fire himself should not presume to alert anyone else. A fully-automated device, home-made but intricate, is best bequeathed to those who need it most. Everything in this little book seems arranged to cope with what threatens it.

No truce is accepted or honoured, so do not hobble yourself by seeking to accomplish it on their behalf. Henri Gaudier-Brzeska spoke to thunder and made the first drafts of almost every painting and sculpture others would produce over the next 50 years. Young enough to think war would give him more life, every part of his promise destroyed him.

Instantly thwarted upon deployment, some theories can survive only in a place where there are not any circumstances. Like a scale model, the theory does not behave like the real thing – the weight, speed and density are off. It's not exactly a lie but at best a slant rhyme. Parables work something out in the privacy of another problem, while children's cautionary rhymes exaggerate consequence so that, for instance, patting a stranger's dog will surely make your legs explode. The feeling of cause-and-effect power this gives a child is short-lived. Rational motive also misleads. An adult learns that many things can happen impartially to end the Earth.

The best writers of fairy tales understood that life is bones in treacle and that treacle is expensive. Hans Christian Andersen, a creepy writer whose potential readers have been kept at bay for decades by Danny Kaye's stupid face, wrote in *The Shadow* about an honest author whose shadow detaches and becomes a 'man of the world', learning the twists of human society. Finding great success, it enslaves the meek author as its own shadow, and finally has him executed. In Wilde's *The Fisherman and His Soul*, a witch claims that the fisherman's shadow is his soul and this he cuts away with a knife so as to live in the vividly fertile undersea world of his beloved mermaid. The shadow asks for the fisherman's heart but is refused, and so the shade sabotages the fisherman's life of love and beauty. The shadow, when apart, is as malignant as the one in Andersen's tale. The loving heart, senses and mind are treasured, and it seems that the witch lied about the shadow being a soul. In Japan they call intuition 'stomach art'. A man was once tasked with creating something using only the stomach contents of a great white shark. The result resembled a kind of consultant. It's pathetic to have someone else's gut feeling.

8

THE THIRD CLOWN

*"Any good insolence accommodates
whole universes."*

I WAS DOING A STORY ABOUT A CHILDHOOD visit to the circus and wrote 'They pounced, two clowns holding me by the arms while a fourth beat the bejesus out of me.' I found this mistake of the missing third clown very funny but didn't know why. When the mind has to jump a gap, the spark it fires can tickle the brain's surface or ignite unused pathways, depending on the guidelines placed on either side. The musician Thelonious Monk was frustrated that the fractional and hybrid tones he heard in Indian music were not on his keyboard, so he struck the keys on either side to suggest them. Poets use the same dodge by staking images on either side of a feeling they cannot point to or describe directly.

A large example was pulled off under the state capitalism of the Soviet era, where Mikhail Bulgakov hung helpless between thin wings of obedience. A game of catch and release of the kind played on noticers from Dostoevsky to Tolokonnikova was the least he could expect amid Russia's 'don't ask, don't tell' attitude to the truth. In a rare exception to the policy, Stalin himself phoned to ask Bulgakov if such a valuable thinker really did want to leave the motherland, at which the author understandably shat himself and assured the dictator he'd never considered it. It was in the face of this unctuous imprisonment that *The Master and Margarita* came together. The book has two settings: Soviet Moscow during a visit by Satan and his carnivalesque attendants, and Jerusalem at the time of Jesus's execution, blood-lit like a de Chirico. Rebounding back and forth between these two atmospheres and pondering why they exist in the same book, the reader ends up tasting a space between the two which is *deeply* strange and which could not be conveyed by any other means. Holding his worn body around him like a coat until the book could look after itself, Bulgakov wrote himself into the ground. He was turfed over along with the intuition needed for such very particular settings – an inspiration lacking in later authors who attempted the master's trick. We learn early that apparent opposite extremes are often the same actions performed by different bastards. Some cultures cut off the hands of thieves; Columbus cut off the hands of the Bahaman Indians he stole from. But working with seemingly unrelated extremes is a glass key you must turn very carefully. Done right, it puts sherbet in the heart and washes a purple-white feeling through the top of the brain.

Write three sentences and remove the middle one – often the deleted sentence is implied by the remaining material. This is great for satire, as when readers fill in the gap, they think it's their idea. But too loose a gap and it crowds with confused speculation. Even looser and it's empty. There is an alternative cosmic finale theory that the universe will continue expanding and diluting, dissipating out of existence – another fine end after so much particularisation. And we have seen that the universe seems to want difference and divergence but doesn't necessarily reward it. That's no reason to expend energy creating emptiness. There is plenty.

Some have used this deliberate halfwaying of disclosure as a skip code against moronic observers but it's best as a compression tool. Chamfort's aphorisms were so cumbersome he had them brought in on a spit. But you can tell a story in two words – for instance: 'Ears, goodbye.' Compression honours the reader. If two ideas are the same shape you can flow from one to the other mid-idea and find that an impossible distance has been covered – you've folded space. When the relationship between the ideas has integrity, they accelerate each other – when not, you're pulling a fast one and people know it. Many words become specifically-bonded through habit despite applying elsewhere – we don't often hear about Australian apartheid. Symbols save space. The odd rigidity of lateral thinkers and the limitations of the amplituhedron can be condensed into the characteristic blandness of a jeweller.

In the age of vinyl it was an occasional treat to nest parallel grooves so that an entirely different record played depending on which spiral the needle happened to drop into. In writing, the same process is called *paronomasia*. It can be used for a dumb pun, a paragraph or a full book. Whole empires have used it in life, their real words several feet under the ground, directly below those used and active in related but unrecognisable ways. Empires and art can also thrive by leaving out any mention of some essential element, like someone bungling a joke. Delmore Schwartz believed the only way to understand *Hamlet* was to assume from the start that all the characters are roaring drunk. Many people have suggested that *The Importance of Being Earnest* takes place in a lunatic asylum – the inspiration, perhaps, for its lock-in twin *What the Butler Saw*.

Partial knowledge can polarise opinion. Scholars insist St George didn't kill the dragon, which means either it never existed or it's still out there. What's left out may relocate. All the 13th houses and hotel floors are heaped in a single town where no-one is superstitious and most are happy. In Florida an old guy found he was treated with strange respect at a certain diner and would be left alone to dine *gratis* and for nothing so long as he accepted that everyone called him Joe. One day he went in and was beaten to a pulp by the entire crowd. Months later he'd recovered enough to notice that the day before the incident, Joe DiMaggio had died.

But because this set of manoeuvres is enabled by the material, you may find that the more you put in, the smaller the piece becomes. It concentrates into a honeycombed oyster, a pearl in every cell. In art this has extruded the crammed schematics of Adolf Wolfli, Joseph Grebing, Augustin Lesage and Paul Laffoley. Their style of rich lozenged consoles of information first appeared in the historically expunged genre of loaded puzzle paintings which fluked up amid the regal gloom of Tudor England and was almost immediately choked off for its unseemly colour and conceptual horseplay. One of the few that survived is a portrait of Christopher Hatton from the workshop of William Segar around 1580. It would be centuries before such ineptly rendered scorpions would be seen again. Schematic art informs the sort of book which, rather than being read narratively, is viewed in one hit from above. When things at a distance are as sharply visible as those close by, the sum of information is as intense as a heart attack. Space has no edges and no use for calculation. But as a point in space, a book which is an example of its own arguments is a good use of the dimensions available.

Another potential compressor is a system of multiple framed narratives which plummet leagues deep, as in Catherine M. Valente's lush *Orphan's Tales* series. Fun has been had level-jumping and slyly marooning the reader one dream under – all tricks performed in *The Manuscript Found in Saragossa*. Strangely though, many writers take the frame structure as licence to sprawl rather than shape a precision-fitted vortex that peels the reader in one long spiral.

There's a limit to the number of times a piece of paper can be folded but not to folds of information. It will want to unpack fast, however, its every atom serving as an accelerant to every other. The miniaturisation necessary to carry the payload makes it extremely rich. There are strange side-effects, such as the multiple re-superimposing of characters over themselves resulting in seraphized figures, from the Pierre et Gilles saints of Genet to the E-number angels of Francesca Lia Block. Even the connective tissue glitters. Characters should be as special as Hindu gods, each the most intense at the time you are with them. Banana Yoshimoto places ghosts in her lines but an examination of where exactly they are concealed reveals nothing. Thomas Ligotti does something similar but is generous enough to drop a few clues by mentioning *Gas Station Carnivals* or the *Dream of a Mannikin* as possible sources of his idiosyncratic heebie-jeebies. Strangely enough, the clown in Ligotti's boutique fright *The Clown Puppet* is a dead ringer for the one I lost from my story. For a clown, stark terror is the coin of the realm and that beautiful bastard knew the Ligotti gig was better value.

Compression and direction of force are key in getting the full effect from your work. The shape of the piece determines its over-all arc of projection, as when a broad base of assumptions propels the sharpest elements away from it in a wide span. The environment itself, if rigid, can often add to compression and so to the subsequent force of an incendiary charge. How to punish those who declare that Putin is 'not Russia's first gay leader'? In Turkey, publishers present books of banned authors to the state prosecutor and demand to be prosecuted. This sort of bluff-calling is equivalent to satire which takes an argument to its absurd end. The letter of the law blurs the more a jail's bars come into focus.

Many sages advise against a surprise ending but fail to say where the surprise should be. Do they mean a story should include nothing we don't already know, or that the whole thing should be a surprise? The tension in many tales derives from the certainty, throughout, that it's about to kick off and do something. More often than not the tension remains. Lovecraft's stories, constructed like anecdotal jokes in prose purple as a Valentine liver, rely on a gradual realisation of the unbelievable thing about to be revealed and the need to stick around to see if he has the gall to go through with it. And he always does. Clark Ashton Smith used Lovecraft's iconography but didn't use the joke form, making up for this by composing his works from rubies, black gemstones and Martian nectar at the rate of a half-cent per word.

A work with a lot of gears tends to weigh less when in operation than when it's still. But a device with no moving parts simply allows you to find out what it is. Daniel Pinkwater started doing this in books like *Lizard Music*, which he wrote at the apogee of a nimble leap over a cattle fence. Pinkwater is able to spring surprises by having no more idea of what's going to happen than the reader does. When a story falls through you so easily, a casual slip reveals its ability to move on any axis. This diagonal gladdening frees a galore of fauna unaware that its method of delivery was a leopard-print prayer. In nature we find a toad that looks like a scone, albeit an expensive one. The walrus is one of the few animals capable of being both fat and bendy. Though possessing three hearts, your common or garden octopus doesn't show much courage when discovered and flees like Baudrillard, obscuring its escape with a waste of ink. The animal kingdom has much to teach us about delirium and blown time. Would Edouard Martinet's solex-headed creatures of Byzantium enamel play with Shinichi Sawada's spiky crittergods? Clever scale jumping is unnecessary in the double atmosphere of vividly unprejudiced attention and a space so inscrutable it cannot be exploited. And all are naked – some belligerently so.

Readers know the disappointment of a book that looks like a brick but promises ideas, of which a half of one is found within like half an old nail. Ancient storytellers had the practical grace to stick a fork in it before it reverted to carbon. Even the author of *The Tale of Genji*, an 11th-century saga with the open-endedness of a soap, grew weary enough to stop in mid-sentence and drop her pen down a well. One of the great revivers of the novel form, Shikibu also used the quirk of leaving a page blank to indicate the death of a character, a trick taken up by Sterne 700 years later. Inevitably, myths arose about Shikibu's lank-haired writing brush climbing out of the well, intent on continuing the work endlessly.

Standard practice is to start a narrative in the middle, when things are already happening, but starting as events reach a conclusion or their aftermath cuts down on length and hones discipline. Logically the later you leave it the more information you'll cram, so starting after the universe ends should cover all bases, but in practice this disappoints all but the general reader. A median point can result in a conceptual ghetto, like the wishful thinking of 17th-century maps of California Island. In the words of Lizzy Descloux, 'It will stop because it can't catch up with eternity.' It goes deep but in only one location. Brion Gysin recognised this and had fun with it. Like all without power, he could have exchanged his philosophy with any one of his friends without its making the slightest difference. For amusement he changed the order in which the elements of confusion frazzled about him.

There is a popular theory that on the 14th of November 1918 all the objects in the world took one step to the right and no longer matched up with their names, and that humanity adjusted almost immediately as if to daylight savings time. Supposedly this explains why books before that date needed so much watering. It's also claimed that if continual steps in one direction returned all objects eventually to their original names – despite intervening changes in form and the invention of new words – it would prove that spacetime is spherical. In fact the 1918 word-shunt is probably a metaphor for the official declaration of new circumstances and new enemies, and the pretence that it has always been so. This creates the temptation to introduce unauthorised enemies and narratives between declarations and cause a pile-up on the conveyor belt.

Some native Americans had a practice of considering important issues once sober and once stoned, from which a conclusion would be averaged. The closest politicians get to this is a Borisian blizzard of cocaine through which neither black nor grey are visible. This can make it easy to take malice for stupidity or stumble amid their variants. In cases of obvious simplicity a stance of falsely cautious delay is adopted as if to perceive all the subtleties of the affair. In the face of complicated peril a traditional rack of mistakes is called up for quick selection. These are not the short-term stupidities they seem, since a closer look will usually reveal that they profit one or other special interest. It's in the long term that their idiocy spreads into dismal flower. It has been argued that it's pointless to consider future consequence because the future doesn't exist, a position held by most corporate governments and a few religions. In politics, money and bones are what's left after the tide goes out. This blend has saved commerce the annoyance of government bodies asking questions while the grown-ups are talking.

Principles of escalation should result in artworks becoming more effective, and the fact that they are becoming more dilute raises the question of the purpose they are thought to serve. That purpose appears to be insulation. Neuroscientists have stated that the brain operates a system which limits the amount that we have to think, so that we are not required to re-examine everything at all times. But this automation has found common cause with exhaustion and retreat from stress to become the dominant – and in many people the only – system in operation. Repetition maintains the illusion of activity. Some view the same works repeatedly. Lake monsters maintain no consistency in when to appear or what shape to exhibit when they do. A whale impresses every time it surfaces, though roughly the same shape on each occasion. Yet many great works are viewed more for their familiarity than their greatness. New notions are a bother. The decay of vigilance and slackening of contempt have also rendered those afflicted disturbingly available. A doll among the cobwebs in an abandoned half-car has brighter ideas in her head.

Creative legends often have 'missing years' in their biographies – if we take Da Vinci's two, Shakespeare's first four and Moliere's two and plot this against their overall level of creativity, the results are confusing. We can adjust for the fact that Moliere had to deal with a load of Frenchmen or that Shakespeare was covered in mud, but the only correlation would seem to be that of missing years with posthumous fame. Shakespeare had a second set of blank years later on, taking his full total to 11, slightly more than Machiavelli. The fact is that absolute lack of information sends people into a frenzy of speculative compensation and the need to develop a system to explain it – all features of a lopsided economy. These artists may have been doing something for themselves without fanfare or creating their most innovative work, or both – suspicious acts among the living, either are encouraged in the long-dead.

Get a clue and you live surrounded by a secret message, closer than the blood in your hands. You'll find the apocalypse is an odd colour. It leaves you raw enough to hear your reflection granulate across a mirror's surface. Sliding patterns synchronise and re-align many times a minute without conscious grafting or formulae, gestalt coral growing to merge into a burgundy reef of unpopular richness. All this tinkering with dimensional properties results in time dilation and occasional nosebleeds. Too fast a return to the dilute world may leave you turned inside-out like a glove, suffocating inside a closed colour. When writing *Gargantua and Pantagruel* Rabelais thought it wouldn't be a bad idea to include a poem with words missing because rats and bugs had eaten them. Modern editions simply fill them in to remove the only interesting thing about the passage. It's sad to be reminded that blandness is policy. Bob Kaufman was redacted from Beat histories for being often on the street and always black. His works were the colour-treated nebulae of an outlawed space project, rendered in a noise-to-signal euphoria. Busted for being, he sent his eyes away like snails to bring back glints of fiasco and emerged saying more than he knew. One time his head gave off a subway spark, wounding his shoulder. His red footprints led to the stained wallpaper of a solid wall, at which they did not stop. He was through.

9

THE FUTURE IS OBVIOUS

*"Lucifer is a black glove we wear to
hide our own fingerprints."*

Humanity's abhorrence of common sense has a similar quality to that afforded originality because it, too, is a departure from familiar circumstance. The relatively reasonable Greek statesman Solon let himself down by making it a crime to publicly express political neutrality and also a crime to publicly speak ill of the living or dead, in the great tradition of combinatory laws that do not allow people to quite exist. This squeezing forces a soul in one of several directions — suicide, a beleaguered almost-deadness under the law, or a freedom that walks behind the climate. A bust of Solon portrays a slightly dazed man with a beard of broccoli coral. Since those stricken days legislators have competed for our despair by passing hundreds of new laws each time we look away.

Society's harassments are not always deterred by death — some of those guillotined in the late 19th century found their heads being hectored by scientists eager to see if the victim's eyes would swivel at their tormentors. The eyes did respond, fixing the scientists with a stare of stony resolve as if at the last straw. Miscreants of disciplined character sought to bring enough air into the mouth before severance that when the detached head was raised triumphantly to the crowd it might utter a single word. A favourite was 'And?' The regime could no longer coherently deny that decapitation was a false economy or argue that it 'made sure', but the beheadings continued. The notion of it as a heartening public spectacle was not taken up by the Nazis, who performed the procedure in closed gymnasiums. They may have realised that targeting the head was a tacit admission that this was what dissidents were using. Pharaohs of ancient Egypt believed the heart was the seat of the intellect and had it wrapped separately.

Consequences always look inevitable in retrospect, and usually ahead of time too, as the same facts are available in both cases. It's the old spycraft trick of following someone by walking in front of them while looking in a mirror or window reflections. The lucid subject ducks off course.

Repetition is ideal for inducing trance, whether over minutes or years, and consent is honoured less the greater the duration. You can tell time by the cry of 'Never again'. But as knowledge retention is reduced, historical repetition threatens to catch up. If repetition intervals ever become shorter than mass memory, facts will be learned through being too constantly in-your-face to deny. It's been questioned whether such a catch-up can ever happen to humanity, either because memory shrinkage is propelled by fear, or because after acknowledging the obvious we will no longer align with the definition of human beings.

Everyone I know anticipates each economic slump long in advance but it never makes a difference as they don't have any money in the first place. Consequence is more visible to those who are not invested. But who would expect a government to be so cruel as to throw the non-wealthy under the bus? I would. So would you – it's okay to admit it. The future is obvious. Escalating suicide, the 20-year real-terms recession, the blackout, the plagues, those people falling onto the tracks, microhomes and governments' continued abuse of 'emergencies', are obvious. Yet many feel it a duty to portray shock or surprise when it comes along. This faked shock and the time claimed to process and express it are an effective tactic to delay action. The energy expended on remaining re-surprisable is gigantic. Human beings aren't content to cast reason aside – it has to hit someone. The war on non-state terror by definition excepts the sort of 'lively terror' once favoured by Churchill in using poison gas against recalcitrant tribes. Fire-bombing has been effective from Tulsa to Shanghai but what its effect has been is understood simultaneously in retrospect and in regard only to the short term. When one excitable politico stated that 'The Jews should tremble before us, not we before them', the possibility of neither trembling seems not to have occurred to a man whose insecurity, corkscrew reasoning and inability to use his 'inside voice' has him indelibly branded Our Lady of the Shortbread.

Historians like Tuchman and Maier make a point of not mentioning an outcome until its proper moment in the story, and in real life people who know the ending are ignored for the same reason – retaining the chance of diversion and feigned surprise. In addition to the avoidance of pseudo-spoilers, people like things to happen in a comfortable narrative order, necessitating that certain ideas and inventions be ignored for decades, centuries or millennia.

The coelacanth, a dinosaur fish thought long extinct, became a media sensation when fishermen caught one in 1938. Known for its Clanger armour and merry smile, the coelacanth is now thought to bestow luck on those who catch it, especially those into whom it sinks its needle-like teeth. Yet what if it had never been thought obsolete? Sailors would probably kick it away with a bitter curse, calling it 'the mudlark of the sea', or 'Mary'. An idea can also be a Lazarus taxon which re-emerges after apparent extinction, but in this case its first appearance is denied. Michael Reynolds' earthships are like something out of *Myst*, cheap as sea glass and as beautiful. Off the grid and solving every ecological housing problem, their lack of fame is a result of unwavering efforts by lobbyists and regulators. Zero-footprint architecture simultaneously provokes the accusation of outdated hippiedom and the protest that it is unprecedented. When such an idea is deemed to have learned its lesson and is freed from its baffling confinement, no time is wasted discussing why it was put away or how a repeat of such dead centuries might be avoided. The unspoken hope is that nothing has been lost during its neglect and that it is still viable for exploitation, like the ice-preserved structure of an obsolete pathogen. The idea of black holes was put forward in 1783 by John Michell and in 1915 by Einstein. Global electromagnetic resonances were accurately calculated by Tesla in 1899 and by Schumann in 1952, upon which they were called Schumann resonances. Also lost to memory for several decades were Richard Semon's theories on the effective retrieval of memory, including the stimulation of a previous and similar memory imprint or 'engram'. An original idea will find no similar engram.

The greatest single time of mass re-discovery has been called the Renaissance, but the disinclination to recover ideas suppressed since then has led to its being re-named the 'early modern' period in a sad attempt to share in its distant credit. This echoes the UK's attempt to conceptually fill the massive gap between rich and poor by stretching the very wealthy across the expanse and rebranding them the middle class.

To be neither surprised nor resigned is the work of a living brain. In addition to direction, another trick of the human eye is its convincing the mind to always have a point of focus, which requires the attention to waste energy darting around. Bilateral organisation in the brain can result in a fluttering in the chest or head when stimuli cross the midline. The halves of the brain are shaking hands at the border. Those without bi-lateral organisation have re-distributed brain functions so that something compelling might be assigned to the area that would normally coordinate slapping a squirrel in the face, not to mention the dumb surprise at it flying sideways into a hedge. Mindgasms are multiplied in a brain glittering with boundary fragments. Like the compound eye of an insect, a compound brain can focus on a bunch of things at once. This allows the mind to perform a fractal dive, pouring through everlasting data assemblages, each level a *wimmelbild* or teeming scene with equal detail everywhere. In this order of operation, pattern recognition is easy. Luckily, function reassignment means the human brain does not have to physically segment like cell division over an evolutionary timescale. A mind can be organisationally fissioned by music, a book or movie, if they're built for that.

But such chicanery should not be necessary to notice dead-regular historical beats, and there are perils. The marine brittle star's use of its entire surface as a compound eye suggests the notion of distributing brain function throughout the human body. Their tendency to jettison their senses when anything attempts to detain them is the act of a sophist, but they often survive. One sophist was Cratylus, whose oscillating maxims had people wanting to whop him to death with an oar. It's possible to use contradiction to herd and funnel an audience but that wasn't his intention. He was tired of defining every fluctuating word as he went along and stopped speaking, merely moving his finger occasionally. The finger conveyed little meaning and was not jettisoned in his lifetime.

Much has been made of Morgan Robertson's book about the voyage of the *Titan*, a massive passenger liner which hit an iceberg and sank in the same location and circumstances as the *Titanic*. Published 14 years before the *Titanic*'s maiden voyage, it has been questioned whether this was divination or coincidence. In fact it merely stated the obvious outcome of a massive, complacently-captained ship with few lifeboats hitting an iceberg in an area known for them. It wasn't even creative. Regarding infinity, Giordano Bruno had no scientific evidence to point to except the sky and the look of thirst on his own face. His acceptance of the self-evident freed up the large amounts of energy needed to survive torture and burn brightly at the stake.

Cleve Cartmill was one of the last on the bandwagon when his humdrum 1944 story 'Deadline' discussed an atomic weapon, but his description of methods to separate uranium into fissionable and non-fissionable isotopes – a problem being scrutinised by the secret Manhattan Project – had security agents paying him a visit as fast as their arms and legs could take them. Cartmill directed them to publisher John W Campbell, who had to explain patiently that the question was obvious to anyone with a physics background. Even in 1931 a nuclear device was a relatively bland MacGuffin for Harry Stephen Keeler, whose plot ideas were so original but whose writing was as indigestible as a helicopter, and of whom one critic complained: 'Mr Keeler writes his peculiar novels merely to satisfy his own undisciplined urge for creative joy.' His obsessions with clowns, skulls and midgets recall the worst excesses of Roosevelt's New Deal.

It's a cliché that with our future ahead of us and our past behind, a manoeuvre to the sides, above or below might expose epic sweeps of terrain to explore, each sideline having different properties and climates. There is one which is made entirely of interwoven targets, one which is a giddy chaos of pop-rocks, one in which everything in one direction is a euphemism for everything in the other, one which is all soppiness and jumper cables, one which is sacred and unbearable, one across which visitors are ricocheted a universe-depth twice per standard second, another where the coincidences are piling up, and yet another which is all and everywhere solid unliveable gemstone without even light to clarify the explanation which stripes it as through a stick of holiday rock. Borges used one of these as a cupboard. But less often discussed is the fact that in the dense spindle of systems which project at perfect right angles from time, progress through them sees past, present and future growing distant at the same rate and for this reason travellers of these vertices joke a lot about death. At oblique vertices from the present, the past and future recede at different rates. We can add the factor of setting off from a point other than the present, and of travelling back and forth along our alternative vertices so that we cross over the traditional timeline like an overpass. Can we jump from one sideline to another? From one rod of a spindle to another, orbiting normal time? How far out do the vertices go? Past and future are a crummy set of limitations, the last couple of turkeys in the store window. This took about a minute to think up by ducking down a sideline where I can be a clever wanker and get away with it. There's also a crane fly the size of a giraffe, a party of vacationing yellow demons and a blood swamp growing trees that are plated like the tails of lobsters. And the sea, on the sunny day you find it, exists just to see the look on your face.

It's been argued that audiences do not appreciate some art for what it is until at some point in the future they blunder into the mindset in which it was created. This can also operate against the work, as in the worldwide instant when everyone realised Jeff Koons was shit.

There may come a future where human beings have been eroded smooth like the face of a coin and a hero unearths a fossilized moped in ruined centigrades. There may even come a time when authorities cease to pretend surprise and disappointment at the results of their policies. What would be the first clues that this had happened?

10

THE STITCH-UP

*"The most amusing thing about a pantomime horse
is having to shoot it twice."*

THE STORY IS STILL TOLD THAT CARLOS Castaneda heard of the Aztec god Quetzalcoatl and mistakenly worshipped an axolotl, an antlered albino tadpole the size of a parsnip. For two years the cute smile of the drifting creature convinced him he was onto something, until he realised he was projecting and turned his gaze to a broader screen. The story is challenged because, after all, who could believe it? Regardless of the controversy, Castaneda's fakery gave us some of the greatest yarns in the ghost story tradition, reaching a sweet-spot of folk invention in *The Power of Silence*.

The sticky infinity of unformed ideas is so rarely visited by humanity that many notions have assembled themselves in exasperation and crowded forward for easy access, with free offers to attract the attention. Like brewers' fruit left so long on the branch that it begins to ferment itself, the merest touch brings them into your hand. They are often so crass they can be nudged into the visible by the randomised combination of existing ideas, yet though requiring the absolute minimum of creativity, these easy pickings are generally ignored or bungled. Cryptozoologists love telling the tale of the carny who stitched a blowfish and a bat together, only to find he had created a lawyer. Many buildings in Helsinki have the colour, design and perforation pattern of a Rich Tea biscuit, which was presumably what the architect's eye happened to fall upon when trying to think of something new. The precocious phrase 'They won't be expecting this' proved sadly prescient.

Yet slip-ups happen, and we sometimes forget to evade those most obvious of original ideas which take any opportunity to present themselves. A now-famous artist accidentally folded a shirt in an impossible direction, lifting an extradimensional tent-flap which allowed several suspended curios into the basement laundry room. These bulging artefacts were slivers of a single higher-space object which, when reconstructed by topological extrapolation, appeared to be a seated farmer wearing a T-shirt bearing the phrase 'Nature is not a river that flows behind our backs'. The artist's subsequent career stretched the meaning of this phrase beyond the limits of measurement. It wasn't much, but it was something.

While the truly original go unimpeded by monuments, others travel in people's shadows, attached to their shade like pilot fish. The writer Albert Paine possessed several fragments of Mark Twain's unfinished work *No. 44* and through apparent creative intoxication re-wrote large parts of it, publishing the result under Twain's name as *The Mysterious Stranger*. Twain's manuscripts were examined after Paine's death and a more faithful version of *No. 44* was produced. It's disconcerting to find that Paine's version is more imaginative and satirically focussed than Twain's. Paine's experience is similar to that of established authors who free themselves up by taking a pen name, or McAuley and Stewart's invention of Ern Malley to hoax the Australian poetry scene and their realisation that some Malley passages were actually pretty good. Writing wants to be good. It wants to be free to be good.

But those who fear originality – or fear the results if they try for it – flop on the chicken-bone pillow of the tried, deciding that the best we can do is refine the design. As far as I know, no profits from *The Hunger Games* went to Koushun Takami, or from *Inception* to Yasutaka Tsutsui. Will Banksy pay a fee to Arofish? These sloppy Trelawneys save the body and leave the heart, the mischief and moral centre that powered it. Without such a centre, satire can work for a little while like a squid valve, propelled by what it casts behind, but without direction. If Mark Leyner's candy assortments were put at the service of something, he would have wrong-footed readers rather than allow them to get his zany number with no surprises.

In *American Psycho*, Ellis pretended to say what everyone knew already about consumer society, but when trying to embed what he really meant he found he didn't know whether to shoot a cake or kiss an ostrich. He gave up, leaving only the decoy, a husk which met with great success and was taken as a standard template for the modern novel. To believe it went otherwise is to accept that he was a conscious fraud. Perhaps if a book is entirely empty we shouldn't feel bad about filling it.

There can be wheel-spinning fun in taking the style of a previous work and outstripping its content. The first rule of *Fight Club* – you do not talk about *The Day Philosophy Dies*. Carlton Mellick III collected a tissue sample from the body-horror portion of Burroughs' schtick and grew it into a gutty and glistening career, atop which his own chin projected like a keep. Kafka was painstakingly checking that every single word he wrote was turned in the same direction long before he took *Little Dorrit*'s Circumlocution

Office and made it his own. His inevitability machines sometimes filled him with a fiendish glee and when he read his work aloud to friends he was often helpless with laughter. It takes stamina to make a book with one flavour all the way across like a ceramic brick wall.

Artists derive warmth from fantasies of civilisation destroyed by flood, asteroid or the right idea. Richard Jefferies' post-apocalyptic *After London* of 1885 saw England overgrown by nature and swamped cities yellow with poison gas. While HG Wells would later draft in some aliens with three shoulders and no mercy, the cause of Jefferies' apocalypse is far in the past and the world has become *Stalker*'s Zone. Some scenes have the creepy strength of 40 beaked elephants. Wyndham took *After London* and added some easily-killed walking flowers – survivalism for dweebs – in the fun *Day of the Triffids*. JG Ballard took it and wrote *The Drowned World*, adding nothing. The movie *28 Days Later* copied *Day of the Triffids* point for point, but wryly replaced triffids with average London residents whose typical behaviour the unworldly hero attributes to a zombie virus. In a way this took things full circle, recalling Jules Verne's 1863 book *Paris in the Twentieth Century*. Verne's editor rejected the book, saying nobody would believe that fax machines could ever exist or that waiters could ever be so rude. By the time the manuscript was rediscovered in 1989, reality had surpassed Verne's vision and the average capital city was a 24/7 apocalypse unsuited to sentient life. The literary carpetbaggers who descended on Paris in the 1920s never foresaw that their meaning would be changed by revisions to the world's cipher key, even as they asked about the wireless in their hotel. Fitzgerald wrote a book that died soon after publication but continued to fool people because its hair and nails kept growing.

A challenge is presented when an idea or genre appears to reach its outermost limit, as in Greg Egan's stunning *Diaspora* – though in that case no one has taken up the challenge and cyberpunk now reiterates in its own shallows. It's been around long enough that people like Lovelace felt wretched for being only a century of sunrises ahead. Alfred Jarry's cyborg sex book *The Supermale*, written in 1901 before anyone could stop him, begins as a mannered conversation piece and ends with the hero having sex 82 times in one day and escaping from a melting love machine, dying tangled in metal. Loose talk about electrodes was less acceptable in those days and Jarry walked bent like an elbow under the shelter of neglect and rain. His honesty is particularly noteworthy and unexplained. This marginal dynamo worked between wars and died before the fear-forged intelligence sump that followed, an event known in scientific circles as a 'dolt spike'. Jarry himself invented pataphysics, 'the laws governing exceptions', when people had just been starting to like him. Basically it was a position paper for mayhem and monkey-shines. Where others saw a couple of sea urchins, Jarry saw a call to adventure. He had a pulmonary brain which beat so hard it jolted his head, producing several plays about the infantile Ubu, a skittle-shaped tyrant with a hunger-spiral on his belly. Those who didn't understand it apologised on its behalf. Ubu was later the model for the globe-headed protagonist in *Kure Kure Takora* (*Gimme Gimme Octopus*), the 260-episode TV epic about an octopus whose thirst for power leads him into the drawbacks of tyranny, theft, betrayal and occasional rampages of unbelievable violence. Something failed is not necessarily something dead, and Jarry's failure was so complicated it still has its own functional metabolism. His ideas are raided by those who don't even bother to switch the plates and who sometimes feel rebellious as they test the pointless fencing of variants.

Today, among those who think that paper is the dead skin of magic, many don't believe that early works are real. Hokusai's centuries-old tentacle porn looks like retro-styled hentai. Works that appear closer together in time can require even muddier thinking by disbelievers. The oscillation overthruster in *Buckaroo Banzai* and the flux capacitor in *Back to the Future* take up the same position behind the driver. Doc travels in the fourth dimension and Banzai the eighth. Buckaroo's car first appeared in the treatment *Find the Jetcar, Said the President* in the mid-seventies. The Doc's car was written in the early 1980s. *Buckaroo* was released first by a year and contained several original ideas – but with time travel in the mix, who knows? *Buckaroo* is also notable for such a layering and compression of plot information that some viewers find it incoherent. Important details are mumbled by minor characters off-screen as a dozen visual shenanigans occur higher in the mix. But all the required information is there, and more. Up a few notches, Shane Carruth's *Primer* consists of several spirals nested so tightly you could burn it like a briquette. The information it houses isn't lush, while his subsequent *Upstream Color* is one big swoon smelling of burnt hair and medicine.

Creative genius can crop up anywhere, even – though rarely – in the upper classes. The latter's abnormally high levels of criminality led to hopes of precocious inventiveness from that quarter, but nothing has happened. The well-to-do don't do much. A small change of stance amid the plastic soldiers was exhibited by Pierre Bettencourt, who managed to be a brilliant outsider artist and writer while the rest of his family slumped on the senate and wallowed in financial 'scandal'. Pierre specialised in mixed-media portrayals of Tiki-headed death gods having breakfast and the dream logic of his writing cleared a dappled path for Barry Yourgrau.

Most people settle, like soil over their grave. Even sainthood is standardised on an ironic, pre-chewed planet circled by satellites fitted with quotation marks. Lives are as sad as an angel's dealer, carried away in the woozy gloom of group enthusiasm. Though a blessed relief, Burning Man's briefness and homogenous flavour grieves those who gauge a culture's richness by its points of concentration. There are movies, books and nations that we like enough to wish they were better. But interventions are met with incomprehension and hostility. There's no point waiting for civilisation to raise its game to one in which someone like Kris Saknussemm is the pulp baseline and Kuzhali Manickavel is read as chick-lit. We can spectate the tragic squander of artists who do nothing with their freedom. Bowles's characters navigate the world by planned collision and gravity, her *Two Serious Ladies* unaware of the street hazards of undisguised curiosity. She established a template still used by those who appear to be escaping while being directed as much as anyone when walking atop the maze's walls – from books and movies in which we must sleepwalk with reactive nimrods to videogames in which none of the options are close to what we would do. For those who want their characters inside-out and electrified, Jack Vance's are resourceful and self-directed, Delacorta's languidly wired and self-controlled, and Haushofer's *The Wall* is as much a relief as her character's circumstances would be to anyone sane. But for the real thing, you may have to do it yourself. Hero worship is like misheard lyrics – they are never as good as you thought. Kiss the eyes of your donor once and move on. Imitation is creepy.

11

HEADS WILL ROLL

"It's not rebellion if they just sold it to you."

THE PARABLE OF THE GREAT BANQUET, in which the diners' arms are splinted and fitted with forks four feet long so that they cannot reach the food up to their mouths, leads to the obvious solution of the diners feeding each other and then hunting down and punishing whoever set up this diabolical torture so that it cannot happen to others. After all, they're armed. But though we all think it, I have never seen the 'punishment' phase of the operation suggested in print. Our manners make for tragedy. The same dulling of character that ensures people turn upon each other instead of an oppressor also ensures their subsequent explanation doesn't have much reach.

Virgil suggested there's yelling in Hell but it's hard to summon such chutzpah in a vacuum, or to spark the transforming liveliness of flames. Those infrequent revolutions we do have tend to install some of the same four or five thousand personality types as the old regime, nothing outside this limited pool being accepted. System is irrelevant when those at the helm are fez-wearing toothfish who treat their own principles like a bouncy castle. It's like Bill and Joan Burroughs repeatedly raking the same lizards off the same tree.

In another famous fable, a scorpion asks for a ride across the river on a frog's back, arguing that he wouldn't sting the frog because that would also be killing himself. Halfway across the river the scorpion stings the frog and both go under. A Talmudic telling has the scorpion conveyed without stinging the frog but then killing a fella strolling by on the other shore. In a Persian version an obliging turtle allows the burden's stinger through her tough shell. All scenarios are remarkable for the frog carrying the clever scorpion with nothing to gain and much potential harm from the scorpion, which can survive underwater for several days. The blithe lack of reciprocity is accepted by the English, a people with many bosses to feed and placate. But elsewhere too, the system's defenders assert that it works on an assumption of benevolence. Such benevolence finds no support in observed phenomena. Our ordinary measures of hypocrisy fail us before the operations of government and modern commerce. The sheer proportions of the racket discourage morality.

They'll charge you for being fully inside a room with both legs, while issuing regular edicts as to what must be unthinkable or incomprehensible and what is the decreed emergency in the meantime. There's no reason why inequality should be any less effective than individually contacted victims. In our more lucid instants we know this is wrong as a ham-coloured piano.

The Soviet principle of employment-as-identity now being applied in the West is the logical conclusion of economics theology grafted over the very short political spectrum beloved of most human beings. A good theory, but try to get it above three miles an hour and see what happens. Capitalism is not a symmetrical affliction. Too often it depends on coincidence and a justice we know of only by report. Should we be more careful amid order or amid chaos? Rand used sustained sleight-of-hand equivalencies as in an optical illusion, and while many people fail to notice all that has been left out to make the composition balance, others don't call attention to it. By these means they maintain the mullet of philosophies.

Locked-room murder mysteries ask the question of how the victim was killed in a seemingly unbreached room locked from within. To whodunnit addicts laying around in a clue-induced stupor, considerations of power in the universe at large are muted by attention to the absorbing details and parameters of the room, just as 80 years of a human life may pass without seeing its own context. Old people aren't automatically wise, though all are adept at a judgemental stare as if apprised of souls, even when they're only thinking about the beans on toast they're having later. But the eroding effects of time will remove all cultural ornamentation unless distractions are added regularly via the flux and deflux of fashion. Circumstances are not changed but garnished by elections or, as many call it, 'buffoon renewal'. Years evaporate while quarrying for substance in a society which has forfeited its right to be taken seriously. A billion souls are taken for a ride and made to pay for it, including company cops and the grand project of building a third tier onto the justice system. At the behest of strangers they exist plucked and feeble, depleted by betrayal. Hope is not detrimental to this handy fatigue – it keeps people working in the dream that if they endure these agonies in the correct sequence it will trigger a reward.

These are notions as over-used as a hermit crab with its arse in a tuba and those who restate them must take on a martyrdom of embarrassment. They look adolescent to a species deeply involved in its first attempts at cool. This saturative *helterpolitik* depends on the idea that everything social moves toward habit and system. A fascist nation is one which has forced itself to a conclusion. In Ionesco's *Rhinoceros* almost everyone turns into truculent rhinoceri; in *Invasion of the Body Snatchers* almost everyone becomes eerily complacent celeries. The first plays into people's base desire to conform, the second their resigned surrender to conformity, both driven by fear. Dali liked rhinoceri and saw them emerging from the rocks, perhaps because in Franco's Spain, they were. We can't choose our dictator any more than we can choose who we fall in love with. The Historical Memory Law enacted after Franco's death rejected the legitimacy of his 40-year regime retrospectively, in lieu of a time machine and a taser. The right of the people to alter or abolish a government and set up a new one, endorsed by Thomas Jefferson, had the stated aim of ensuring their safety and happiness. Jesus's strategy, as quoted by Origen from an early version of Matthew, went that 'If they persecute you in this city, flee ye into another; and if they persecute you in the other, flee again into a third.' It's unclear which of these principles Jefferson was following when he forcibly relocated Native Americans. The several occasions of Jesus running away from threatening situations made sense for a man who vacillated between revolution and the only slightly easier road of playing along with prophetic scripture. His suicide-by-cop placed him finally among the Malamatiyya, who take upon themselves the blame for everything, including crimes carried out by others. Most authorities encourage this. Just as K's shame at being subject to the state's edicts cripple him to the point of accepting them in Kafka's *The Trial*, to admit the truth would require action or shame. Keeping the fraud hidden is a collaboration between its victims and those who benefit. A prodded fool can see through the deception to its bland innards – bland because the motive is boring and the method is crass over a large scale. Defenders of the Bible claim there are no accounts of Jesus' teachings in the 40 days after his resurrection because he couldn't stop laughing. But he seems to have mostly sat around speaking in monosyllables. If this was Jesus, he appears to have lost his flare. In fact once the narrative was entirely out of his hands he became the all-purpose Swiss Army Christ we know today.

Sustained resentment was a precursor to the modern calendar. Revolutionaries have been putting on preparatory warpaint for so long, many have suffocated. Most elect to keep their rage safely online, just as the most innovative and beautiful architecture is allowed expression only in videogames. Others pretend they are being merciful to their oppressors – better that than acknowledge impotence. Debord settled for telling the truth above the roar of luxury. Many make do with

China Mieville, quite simply one of the science fiction writers in the UK. Extreme sport, one of the passive traditions, serves as a field bandage for monotony by venting energy and profitless screams into the upper air. Fierce as a radish in the ground, all serve to change the window rather than the view. Upon perking up, they are generally intent on turning the tables 360 degrees. Blame is a bird happy to perch anywhere. The poet Andre Chenier was guillotined for sitting around eating an orange in the wrong house. Legend has it the mob played football with his head for several minutes before realising that no one knew who was on which side. Voltaire was not the revolution's father but served as a placenta to one small rebellion. It took his devotees 10 years of missed beats to accept he was really dead and wouldn't be doing it for them, and a further 10 years to fuck it up royally. These patterns persist like those of the knitters at the guillotine. Che Guevara's legend ripened into the dense synthetic classicism of cigar label art.

Yet the freedoms some populaces do have were fought for – always by people outside of government and commerce – and would not exist otherwise. Not everyone has the patience and mental fortitude to struggle and organise over a lifetime for something that should very obviously exist already. Articulate noticers like Bourne, Russell and Debs – or Peggy Duff who protested the post-war concentration camps in Britain – were among those who commented simply by presenting. Hogarth's works were not satire but early experiments in photography. It's said that by late life the lines of his forehead were so elaborate in character he simply blotted the area with ink and slammed it forward onto a sheet of paper. These 'scorn stamps', surely impossible to authenticate, fetch a pretty penny among connoisseurs of the passive aggressive. Oppression burlesques such as Ngugi Wa Thiong'o's *The Wizard of the Crow* work on a similar principle, crowding together scenes of goons under pressure, dregs in police motley, coercion lacking exuberance and sycophancy intense enough to drive mutation, all at play in the polluted waters of nationalism. Certain vampires are said to be particularly active on St George's Day. To kill one you must cut out and split its heart, nail it in the forehead, shove garlic in its mouth, smear it with lard and dump it in a trench. Coincidentally, this will also kill a human being.

In the Chinese board game Go, some stones are alive, some dead, and some 'unsettled'. The unsettled are not uncollapsed waves in the quantum sense but soldiers whose lives a leader has claimed as its own and whose fate is not decided yet, or the cat in Schrodinger's faulty fantasy, who obviously knows whether it is alive or dead but whose views are deemed irrelevant. Not all battles are fought to be won and there are those who profit financially irrespective of the outcome, greeting the survivors with tilted heads and terminology. Neither the confessions between wars nor its heroes are any recompense. Art never won any wars, nor started any. Peace is not often spectacular. Elaborate compromises become superfluous as forced tolerance gives way to plain comprehension. Nothing to hide on either side, nothing to fear.

The bull was once treated as sacred because it might jab you with a horn or snort suddenly in your ear when you were least expecting it, adding to the many stresses of early civilisation. But the ancient Egyptians, capped by spectacular authority, learned enough about that condition to worship cats due to their casual imperviousness to orders or approval.

Many argue that long ago the interpreter between intention and practice went inconspicuously insane. But the notion of an institution being 'corrupted' sneaks through the assumption that it was not structurally designed to do what is referred to as 'corrupt'. Early humans created language by voicing the synesthetic sound-shape of the object they referred to, a direct process requiring no calculation. Many words retain these shape matches despite massive drift and decay. Synesthetically the word *wolf* presents a wolf whether you've ever seen one or not. But spoken and written language reduced the synesthetic state in humanity so that many people now think in sentences – and not often their own. Some scholars believe malice played a part and that the prehistoric impulse toward spoken language was the desire to be able to lie. Hundreds of landlines came crawling up the beach.

Those who still perceive synesthetically may tend to take people at their word, such as the woman told to repay her debt to society who did so by embarking on a trail of scorching vengeance, or the man who heard for the final time the advice to 'turn that frown upside down' and did so by dropping headfirst out of a window. There are many ideas of what the Singularity may be and one candidate is the emergence of a genuine democracy somewhere in the world. The energy released by such an event might resemble nothing before it. But unlike the fabled discovery of a new colour, it would require no new terms.

12

TOTAL CATASTROPHE WRITING

"The great thing about being ignored is that you can speak the truth with impunity."

WHEN THE GIRL SAID RUMPELSTILTskin's name, he took hold of his leg and whipped it upward, tearing himself in two and spraying his audience with gore. It's rare today to find such commitment to a verbal contract. A promise is a mere curio and words are filmy drifts signifying nothing, so it seems good sense to go through life saying whatever's convenient at the time. A dictator's justifications have so little objective reality they have practically no natural enemies. This psychopathic severance leaves reality to fend for itself and, as always, reality thrives. Sartre wrote of a character who sees a tram full of unlabelled and uncontextualised objects and people. This is fairly easy to induce and is useful as a reminder of what is actually happening. Good artists learn early the habit of stripping the name and context from objects and seeing only their shape, so that disparate objects relate. It's yellow apples and yellow oranges.

This can be a glimpse at scary redemption. The blackest bat has the cutest face. Being alive is past the compass of any pickpocket empire, a plastic rose in its false teeth. Travel shows the effect on the senses of stronger light, longer land and shorter time. But the spectrum of effects created by a mostly self-appointed mind, still and active as a hummingbird, ranges from pure uncut celestial telemetry to that citric itch in the marrow that bothers anyone with a clue and a scram bag.

Paul Scheerbart, whose head began at the wrong end, wrote *Lesabendio* in 1910 when halfway down a waterslide. On an asteroid of rubbery morphons, Lesabendio wants to go further and builds a spire to explore the outer atmosphere, throwing the world off-balance and causing unexpected transformations. His big trip was not outdone for meaning by Foyle's space jaunts in *The Stars My Destination* and makes Dave Bowman's passive Stargate holiday look like a waste of good monoliths. Meanwhile in the 1970s, Rudy Rucker started writing work amok with cartoon biology forced from fluorescent logic spores and stinking like the mirror image of cheese. His work is still some of the most frequently original to break up the desert. He delivers tricked-out fortune cookies from another dimension, bound for quarantine so eat up fast. Each heart-shaped flask of cognitive nectar rotates readers through a tilting sense of buzzy bendspace, causing a sideways vertigo. But he seems to incorporate fizzy Scheerbart architecture and bubble-gum aliens as if piped from the other end of the century by way of Calvino's *Cosmicomics*. Suction-cup guests of this kind are acceptable today. Rudimentary math proved to Scheerbart that he would be decades in the roachy ground before the appropriate time arrived to write his asteroid novel, but he hadn't the grace to wait. And so a bit of experimental-consciousness California slipped out of 1913 Germany. The philosopher Walter Benjamin found *Lesabendio* perfectly illustrated the 'bungled reception of technology' that we allow to shape us and of which I take the Easter Island extinction as an example. All 887 moai statues looked inland, so that the Rapa Nui people had inadvertently created a surveillance society which drove them to a frenzy of judgement and annihilation.

Scheerbart was also an early adopter of the airship as a means of touring a fictional world. The airship has become a shorthand signifier of the alternate world, the skies of other-London or alter-New York clotted with blimps in direct descent from Michael Moorcock's vision in *The Warlord of the Air* and others. As well as coining the term 'multiverse' and writing the most mind-frying fractal chase scenes in his dismissed-in-alarm Second Ether books, Moorcock invented the modern age of steampunk (the first age being that of Fawcett, Verne and Wells) – all of which goes rigorously unacknowledged. The butcher Charles Dellschau seems to have lived a whole alternate life in Airship Texas, filling thick scrapbooks with records and memorabilia of the Sonora Aero Club, of which there are no other records. He had moss in his name before anyone investigated. The Henry Darger of steampunk, his cross-versal condition might have inspired *House of Leaves* if Danielewski hadn't already copper-stripped d.a. levy. Perhaps in an alter-world an aero captain rode in a blimp as bright as a cardiac beetle and wrote secretly about the butcher's trade. Was the 75 years between Dellschau's death and his recognition used more constructively in the parallel world? If he was known earlier, would Russia still defeat the Nazis, the Gulf of Tonkin frauds be exposed sooner or Benno Ohnesorg dodge the cop's bullet? The multiverse model has universes budding off fractally, encapsulated like the linked floatation bladders of seaweed. Some Pacific cultures eat bladderwrack with a butter sauce to indicate their position on the matter. An act which accepts absurdity with such ingenuously sarcastic gusto is a tilted cross-sectional state which zings the marrow.

If sustained, this is the 'still point' satirical method working at the level of lifestyle, releasing far more surrounding energy than it expends – another experiment that has no Fourth of July. The ancient Greeks called the avenging Furies 'the well-wishers'. Art confers no power but can express truth, which persists irrespective of mood or law. In summer it's still summer at night. Perhaps in yet another world, art affects change and villains are rendered pure by principled satire. But on the Earth where airships are sparse and suspect?

Upon taking a gander at the state of things in this world, a wise man said: 'It's a good thing it's true, because it's pretty ugly.' After the Colossus of Rhodes toppled it became a debating stage for the issue of beauty versus truth. Since in this case there was no real conflict, it was acknowledged for its beauty and dismantled for its bronze and iron. As to how long the indecision lasted, accounts vary from 3 years to 800. The beauty of house tiling in ancient Alexandria was not what made them perfect for flaying the flesh from Hypatia, her Christian attackers being immune to such crude abstractions. Materialism and the belief in the inevitability of progress, as posited by communist and capitalist doctrine, approach both truth and beauty with all the backbone of a banana. To protect them from the pyres of the Second World War, Norman Lindsay's wife Rose Soady took 16 crates of his paintings to America, where the authorities burned them. Since the destruction of the Library of Ashurbanipal, the burning of books has continued to this day, not only in the US where the torching of Sanger, Reich, Shaffer and Vonnegut went without fuss but in Sri Lanka, Cuba, Israel, Egypt and the UK – the last touched off mainly by elderly people trying to keep warm.

When philosophers speak of 'obstacles' they have in mind a world where a step or two is free of them. This juicy fantasy is the fruit of living in the mind. Meanwhile, heroes can barely raise themselves off the floor. The billions who work of a broken heart move through an acidic exhaustion where sleep is viewed as an indulgence. During sleep we do not work or consume, are not outward-looking, hysterical or entertaining, and are becoming healthier. Many would wish it abolished, in others. Remember, if you pick up a strange book in a dream and read it, it's your copyright. But such books are notoriously hard to bring back whole. Coleridge managed to retrieve ten sunburned sentences before he was interrupted by a hairdresser.

In Arkady and Boris Strugatsky's book *Definitely Maybe*, scientific discovery is blocked at every turn by bureaucratic interference, strange deliveries and spooky women. Similar things happen if you try to obtain a copy of the book. Its characters conclude that the universe is resisting humanity's progress towards powers that will upset cosmic homeostasis. Is this resistance societal or universal? Do the gears of a fractal mesh between different scales or are they just ornamental duplicates? When Einstein chatted with Rabindranath Tagore – from whom the scientist took away an idea for a new, even wilder hairstyle – the poet ignored considerations of scale and reach, claiming that it is a human universe. Yet despite the dewiest mooncalf knowing that the cold injustice of universal systems outpaces any human psychopath, humanity feels it has the luxury to manufacture additional hardship of its own brand. This surplus sorrow has the repetitive quality seen in other areas of the culture and nothing really new has been introduced for 12,000 years.

A thing done despite absolutely everything is a wonder indeed. With near to no time or energy, the creation of anything substantial becomes a long game. This means keeping the architecture of the project in your mind and the flavour of its first conception in your heart, so that on either side of a waste of time it can be called up intact with its continuity uninterrupted. The process is not spectacular. While imprisoned in a Soviet labour camp Irina Ratushinskaya wrote 250 poems on soap, which she memorised and washed away. Discipline is an honest decision maintained across saturative peril to guard and at times convey a precious thing. Panspermia are said to be hardy seeds or spores which have journeyed through space to land on Earth, where most are eaten at once by birds. The rest must live a fine line – to be dull enough to evade a bird's eye and unique enough to be dismissed by the run of humanity. Many lizards and insects have developed extremely bright and complicated colours so as to be discounted by the latter. It's a strange and risky game, to try for privacy without the interference provoked by appearing to. When Twain became terse about human carnage he was treated like a previously delightful gadfly who had suddenly kicked a kitten out of a window. Simone Weil ached with an always-unfashionable honesty about powerlessness and talked early about the 'trickle-down' theory, an idea without an exact counterpart in reality. Surrounded by the automated and menacingly upbeat, she would never let them stake a claim on her mind. She was later portrayed as having a story as sad as a dead girl's glasses. In life a kind of justice pursued her, growing wings on her honesty. And wings, like honesty, are not socially comfortable. Powerful microphones have recorded the cry of a butterfly as it emerges from its cocoon, and those expecting a shriek of pugnacity or joy have had to admit it sounds more like weary resignation. The resurrections of Mothra, the giant butterfly in Japanese kaiju movies, are treated as colourful religious events, glitter falling upon fat children as the fluffy-faced behemoth dries its wings. Cultures without a monotheistic tradition often find themselves in this kind of jam, worshipping a marzipan badger or a pair of clogs they found in the shed. And the lack of dogma is a boon to the wise. Pythagoras believed in reincarnation and stopped someone beating a dog because he recognised in its barking the cries of a friend. A better man would have stopped it upon recognising in its barking the cries of a dog.

It is not known if an organism exists which can continue to put out energy indefinitely while bringing none in. People who care at all about the output of true creatives seem to expect a somewhat *energetic* despair. It's disingenuous to flounce out hoping to be missed, like the Art Strike of 1990–1993 which nobody noticed. But as we have seen, it can go either way – attack or disregard. To ensure the latter, put original thought at the service of truth. This very few civilised souls can abide and they will respond in a frenzy of neglect. A realist like Zapffe provoked so many people to look the other way, he could more or less do whatever he liked. He chose to climb church steeples with grappling gear and smile down like an ape with a secret. Cioran, barricaded against human babble, sat ready to sneer at anyone who breached his room with jaws akimbo. Ernest Becker appears to have worn a Groucho Marx nose, specs and moustache for twenty years, baffling the Pulitzer people who finally awarded the prize to his corpse for *The Denial of Death*.

Originality is less welcome to the mind than the certainty of death, the exception being suicide and the prescribed resolve to find it incomprehensible. When Panait Istrati improved the shining hour by slashing his throat and surviving, Romain Rolland found he could get past the suicide attempt by focusing on Istrati's writing, which had nothing new in it, and helped him to write more. When Istrati began criticising Stalin with zingers such as 'All right, I can see the broken eggs. Where's this omelette of yours?', Rolland's support quietly withdrew. The distaste around death is complicated when artists decide to lark about at the last minute. Jan Potocki carved a silver bullet from the handle of a sugar bowl, had it blessed by a chaplain and then used it to blow his brains out, after drawing a caricature of himself with a stupid nose. Boris Vian died of heart failure while screaming abuse at a movie adaptation of one of his novels. Li Po is said to have drowned while trying to have sex with a reflection of the moon.

Many deathbed laments concern the energy expended in the commotion of laws and our varying strategies to survive them, just as sharks grow and discard thousands of teeth over a lifetime. The honeycomb structure of an elephant's skull protects the brain from the haranguing and abuse of limber opportunists but cannot retrieve the time wasted, nor the strength lost through exasperation. 'Cruelty before kindness' extends to the admiring words finally expressed after the death of a neglected artist, as though their death explains their meaning in detail. The cherry acid fauna of Eugene Von Bruenchenhein were allowed the light of day 40 years after they were painted, the painter thinned safely to his grave.

A patina of age helps. It's said that upon discovery of the 8,000 terracotta soldiers under China's Shaanxi province, one of the figures was doing something interesting. The accounts vary between mere squatting in a sarcastic way to extruding a foliate superstructure from its shoulders on which were inscribed the Zodiac of False Assumptions: that the space occupied by any human body is more interesting than that which is not, that all happiness is the same colour, that after getting worse things will get better, that the world will end when humanity does, that it's a long way to twist to see your own soul and so on. Ignored by the sentinels around it for two millennia, it's now valued above gold in the strange auburn market of antimundane contraband and is reputedly with a private collector in Novosibirsk.

Biological death – the only kind worth bothering with – is met with fighting stances among those who want to dodge it, an urge rarely motivated by a desire for wisdom. Those cadavers-in-waiting glamoured by technology tend to see a future in which tech arrives equally everywhere. It's claimed that advances in science mean the first human to live to 500 years has already been born – if so, he or she was born into wealth and will hopefully use the extended lifespan to mature beyond being a privileged dick. Doris Lessing remarked that human beings do not live long enough to come to their senses. Another great thinker said he'd use additional years trying to read the expression on the face of a trout. What's obvious is that with extreme longevity, some will go mad and some will go sane. If sane, there is a different kind of tiredness which comes with a strong, long life. It is not the feeling that the entire canvas has been filled in. It's the certainty that you cannot force people to look at what you have so far. But given enough time, you may feel every tickle of sap through the planet's intelligence as tiny rushes of understanding are established. It will be a long time coming. When a bunch of pendulum clocks are put in a room together, after a few days those pendulums will be swinging in unison. A single clock brought into the shop doesn't stand a chance of changing the rhythm of the many, or of maintaining its own. But the heart that maintains its own rhythm is rewarded with treasure, the friction of its angle sparking vivid oblique cross-sectional vistas of the systems of the world. This honesty emerges as a social blemish as rich as a sunspot, complete with coronal loops and reconnection events.

Alternative to a longer life is a mind with a long enough exposure to photograph the long truth. From it may sometimes come a good idea the orbit of which is so large its intersection here seems straight and too simple to have a history. Gurdjieff contended that a soul can be created only by consciously intended work, authentic and from scratch, with nothing stolen. In Chapter 18 of *Picnic at Hanging Rock*, withheld from the public until after Joan Lindsay's death, Miranda and her friends encounter – and are still encountering – a solid vortical hole in space around which time is encapsulated. An instant's sight of it solves a lifetime of questions for the maths teacher Miss McGraw. This is an object worth creating. Lindsay, around whom watches and clocks had always stopped, accomplished this object with a long build-up of pressure and a final, partial release.

Strange flavours bleed through when someone's concerns have moved on while using the same old forms. In Tove Jansson's beautiful *Moominvalley in November*, the Hemulen and friends find the

Moomin house empty and decide to wait for the cute family. During this time they have a party and a variety of small meltdowns, and try building a treehouse. Toft, who tells stories to himself, ponders a small deep-sea nummulite who eats electricity and, little by little, becomes like nothing except itself. The creature rises, emerges and gradually swells into a huge visible phenomenon. Toft tells the nummulite, now hardened and bewildered with worldly defences, 'Make yourself tiny and hide yourself! You'll never get through this!' The creature again finds its own element. Toft waits for the family the longest and finally spots the mast lantern of the Moomins' boat far off and approaching like Dylan's riders. There Jansson's final Moomin book ends.

It seems that great things cannot be consummated until all the lies about them have been heard, so let go. Once expressed, your ideas need not be under your protection. One book answers another and we can let them flap and squabble. Rosendorfer's *Grand Solo For Anton* answers the Strugatsky brothers by suggesting that this world is designed to conceive a single book containing everything, from which the next world will be seeded by the only survivor – a man so boring the author had to get rid of everyone else to make him bearable. Joyce's notion of a seed book for the next universe is played out. People are fuel for the book's calculations and their personal ambitions are irrelevant. I suggest that the human world's blocking of individuals' creativity is a sign that it is performing an experiment to which it wants a very particular answer – bad science writ large. Irrespective of authority's declaration that privacy is a suspect luxury, its oddly invested insistence that in our youth we felt invulnerable and immortal rather than exhausted and precarious, its systemisation of a notional process whereby grief and injustice fade over time, its strangely fearful decrees of what thoughts are impossible and events unforeseeable – reality controls the narrative. It was once trumpeted that true theatre extended many miles above, below and beyond the stage, which is a mere letterbox peep at a portion, but Artaud had other information, having sneaked a peak up at the rigging and seen hysterical and constant maintenance. He had begun to suspect trickery when he noticed the absence of his own levels of agony on stage. The selective view does not survive the colourless cure of honesty.

You may continue waiting for the accident to finish, until the day you disappear from your mirror and oxygen can't use you anymore. You will leave the human world as bland as you found it. You may even be famous.

Or take your remaining life in your hands and see how much of it is yours. There was once a man who lived like a moth trapped in a bellows camera, exhausted by worthless prestige. Instead of a heart he had a green toy kennel containing a roasted almond, and his philosophy was an ingrowing slogan, something about a room taking a liking to its own emptiness. He did target practice on porcelain phrenology heads, gave directions in 'clicks', boasted of paying a special tailbone tax, was secretly baffled by his own pets and finally attacked them in panic and release. Cowering in an ambush of frontiers and invoking remnants in place of rumination, his arguments were airtight and fruitless. He was skin stretched over fear. On his final morning he took a quick gander at the renewed immensity above his head and began betraying it afresh.

There was once a girl who was pale and packed as a root. Those who chose to notice her quiet corner saw her complicating by inches until phosphene riches covered every instant of her progress, an ongoing masterpiece. She walks through the falling world sweating alchemy and extruding complex solid eternities, charged particles streaking upward around her. She creates meaning and hides it above the weather.

Those few who genuinely seek originality will be magnetised to your stuff, even without signposts. It's a sure thing when you own the island's only taxi. Intensely creative common sense gives pure answers of a richness which nudges it into a bandwidth of invisibility – to answer to the edge, then over. When we forget the depth of the planet we forget that cities are cosmetic. Every door opens directly onto infinity. But we are dog-tired and dazzled, with heads like stop-lights.

The great dilution, profitable to the very few, will not take us all. Elsewhere in the heart are lush jungles rained on in the heat, and heavy windowed spheres the dark-stained gold of lions. You are the sugar of the Earth. I bless you a blue streak. I hope the bloodbuzz of accelerating vision blurs you into the seraphim blast of reasonable assumption, producing high hours amid the blaze. On the wall your nuclear shadow, a mere outline without depth, will still prove too strange and unpliable for most. And if it ends in screaming as purple-yellow vines grow from gemstone wreckage to brandish what you have done, you can take strength from knowing it was all your idea.

SUBSCRIBERS

DEAR READER,
The book you are holding came about in a rather different way to most others. It was funded directly by readers through a new website: Unbound.

Unbound is the creation of three writers. We started the company because we believed there had to be a better deal for both writers and readers. On the Unbound website, authors share the ideas for the books they want to write directly with readers. If enough of you support the book by pledging for it in advance, we produce a beautifully bound special subscribers' edition and distribute a regular edition and e-book wherever books are sold, in shops and online.

This new way of publishing is actually a very old idea (Samuel Johnson funded his dictionary this way). We're just using the internet to build each writer a network of patrons. Here, at the back of this book, you'll find the names of all the people who made it happen.

Publishing in this way means readers are no

longer just passive consumers of the books they buy, and authors are free to write the books they really want. They get a much fairer return too – half the profits their books generate, rather than a tiny percentage of the cover price.

If you're not yet a subscriber, we hope that you'll want to join our publishing revolution and have your name listed in one of our books in the future. To get you started, here is a £5 discount on your first pledge. Just visit unbound.com, make your pledge and type Original in the promo code box when you check out.

Thank you for your support,

Dan, Justin and John
Founders, Unbound

SUBSCRIBERS

Unbound is a new kind of publishing house. Our books are funded directly by readers. This was a very popular idea during the late eighteenth and early nineteenth centuries. Now we have revived it for the internet age. It allows authors to write the books they really want to write and readers to support the writing they would most like to see published.

The names listed below are of readers who have pledged their support and made this book happen. If you'd like to join them, visit:

www.unbound.co.uk

Jill Adams
Robert Alcock
Mo Ali
Ted Alkins
David Aronchick
Andy Aylett
Charles Baird
Ben Baldwin
Jasper Bark
Jonathan Barlow
Linda Barlow
Jason Bartlett
Jaimie Batchan
Adam Baylis-West
Denise Behrens
Tony Bennett

Kyle Bergeron
Sam Berkson
Count Otto Black
Dr Sue Black
Samm Blain
Amy Booth
Uke Bosse
Tony Brandrick
Thomas Brasdefer
Richard WH Bray
Paul Brazier
Craig Brewer
James Bridle
Joe Briggs
Ben Brilot
Joseph Buckton

SUBSCRIBERS

Catherine Burnett
Andrew Busby
Paola and Christian
　Butler-Zanetti
Joseph Callanan
Xander Cansell
David Carrington
Sean Carroll
Allen Caruselle
Alex Cashman
Justin Cetinich
Dylan Chapin
Peter Charles
Nora Chassler
Roy Christopher
Brendan Chua
Robert Churm
Tim Clare
Tim Clark
Brendan Clarke
Brian Cochran
Chris Coleman
Stevyn Colgan
David Cooke
K.G. Cooke
Quentin Cooper
Bob Corrigan
Nick Cotter
Lindsey Cox
John Crawford
Jez Creek
Anthony Cule

Dalana Dailey
Dan Dan
Mark Davess
Sean Davey
Harald De Bondt
Paddy Doherty
Wendalynn Donnan
Matt Dowling
Gary Doyle
Clyde Duensing III
David Dukes
Ann Dvoretsky
Brian Eagan
Alf Eaton
Neil Edmond
Ben Charles Edwards
Håvar Ellingsen
G Benjamin Ensor
Sam Enthoven
Andrew Fahey
Paul Farrell
Finlay Finlay
Paul Fischer
Molly Flatt
Isobel Frankish
Viscount Dominic Frisby
Alistair Fruish
Tom Fryer
Dave Fyans
Marc Gallup
Penelope Gane
Saffron Gardenchild

SUBSCRIBERS

Tony Gatner
Philip Gelatt
Francis Gene-Rowe
Ian George
T. Ghelani
Davide Ghilotti
Allan Gilmour
Salena Godden
Susan Godfrey
Duran Gökemre
Dave Goodchild
Allen Goodreds
Voula Grand
Tom Grater
Samuel Gray
John Green
Andreas Grønbech
Erik Guttman
William Hackett-Jones
Josh Halil
Anthony Hall
Stephen Hampshire
James T Harding
Mark Harding
David Harford
Harry Harris
Donnie Harrison
Paul G Harrop
Ian Hart
Caitlin Harvey
Joseph Harvey
James Haskin

Edward Hayward
Søren Heinecke
Paul Hickman
E O Higgins
John Higgs
David Hine
Charles Hitchings
Chris Horseman
Matt Huggins
Phil Humphries
Alastair Hussain
International Authors
Tim Irving
Corey J. White
Majeed Jabbar
Gordon Jackson
Mark Peter Andrew Jackson
Martin Jackson
James
Todd Alan Johnson
Ian Jones
Jonlyus Jonlyus
Aidan Kendrick
John Kent
Robert Kiely
Dan Kieran
Wilf Kieran
Chris King
Darren Kingaby
Paul Kingsnorth
Alexander Kitchens
Jonathan Korman

SUBSCRIBERS

Bob Kuntz
David L. Eccles
Lindsay Colleen "Buckshot"
LaCook
Lex Lamprey
Dirk Lange
Duncan Lawson
Jimmy Leach
Tony Lee
Madison Leigh
Jason Leivian
Craig Lewis
Vyvy Lewis
Trevor Lock
Mikael Lopez
Jack Lord
Finnbar Macabee
Anne Maguire
Chris Maloney
Peter Maloy
Chris Manning
Kate Manning
Ian Maslen
Iain Matheson
Jim Matthews
Steve McCavour
Tom McDermott
Gareth McGuire
Carole McIntosh
Alan McKendrick
Oliver McWilliams
Ilija Melentijevic

Clive Mitchelmore
John Mitchinson
James Moakes
Ben Moor
Leah Moore
Peter Morrison
Jim Morton
David Mosley
Tae Sandoval Murgan
Neil Murray
Gus Murray-Smith
Matthew Murrell
Alex Musson
Rhonda Nicholl
Elizabeth O'Hara
Andrew O'Neill
M.C. O'Neill
John Oakes
Becky Ohlsen
Judy Oxford
David Parsons
Brendan Patricks
Tamsyn Payne
Angela Pearsall
Oliver Pickles
Tim Pilcher
Simon Pinkerton
Daniel Pipe
Kewal Rai
William Reichard
Simon Richings
Aaron Roberts

SUBSCRIBERS

Tom Rollins
Greg Rowland
Peter Samaan
Nicole Sarrocco
K P Saunt
Donna Scott
Luz Seamon
Adam Sharpe
Paul Simpson
Emma Slawinski
Lee Smart
Nell Smith
Soli
Suki Spangles
Torbin Spiggot
David Spurrett
Naveen Srivatsav
Bjørn Stærk
Janice Staines
Andrew Steinberg
Donald Stewart
Matthew Stiles
George Stirling
Aug Stone
James Stringer
Declan Tan
Kenneth Teague
Tolga Tez
Gareth Thomas
Ian Thompson-Corr

Rupert Thomson
Danson Thunderbolt
Penda Tomlinson
Matthew Travis
Olli Tuominen
Ben Tye
Johanna
    Vainikainen-Uusitalo
Marcel van Driel
Mirjam Veenker
Ian Vince
Ken Viola
Jacob John Vrieswyk
Jo W
R. Walsh
Jo Walton
Nigel Watson
Andrew Wenaus
Jake West
Tony White
Jennifer Willis-Jones
David Wilson
Pete Windle
Mark Woffenden
Steve Woodward
Jon Wratten
Alex Wright
Robert Wright
Can Yalcinkaya
Chad Youngberg

A NOTE ABOUT THE TYPEFACES

This book is set in Monotype Bembo Book. Originally drawn by Stanley Morison for the Monotype Corporation in 1929, the design of Bembo was inspired by the types cut by Francesco Griffo and used by Aldus Manutius, the great scholar-typographer of Renaissance Italy. In 1495, Aldus used it to print Cardinal Bembo's *tract de Aetna*, an account of a visit to Mount Etna. Not intended to be a facsimile of Manutius' work, Morison's Bembo was drawn to embody the elegance and fine design features of the original but marry them with the consistency of modern production methods so it would work with high speed printing techniques.

The Bembo used here is the new digital version, called Bembo Book, designed by Robin Nicholas and released in 2005. It is slightly narrower and more elegant than other digital versions of the typeface and was drawn to produce a closer match to the results achieved using the hot metal version when letterpress printed.

The drop capitals are ITC Golden Cockerel Initials by Phill Grimshaw from original drawings by Mr Gill.